AMERICAN LEGAL CULTURE, 1908-1940

Contributions in Legal Studies
Series Editor: *Paul L. Murphy*

Law, Soldiers, and Combat
Peter Karsten

Appellate Courts and Lawyers: Information Gathering in the Adversary System
Thomas B. Marvell

Charting the Future: The Supreme Court Responds to a Changing Society, 1890-1920
John E. Semonche

The Promise of Power; The Emergence of the Legal Profession in Massachusetts, 1760-1840
Gerard W. Gawalt

Inferior Courts, Superior Justice: A History of the Justices of the Peace on the Northwest Frontier, 1853-1889
John R. Wunder

Antitrust and the Oil Monopoly: The Standard Oil Cases, 1890-1911
Bruce Bringhurst

They Have No Rights: Dred Scott's Struggle for Freedom
Walter Ehrlich

Popular Influence Upon Public Policy: Petitioning in Eighteenth-Century Virginia
Raymond C. Bailey

Fathers to Daughters: The Legal Foundations of Female Emancipation
Peggy A. Rabkin

In Honor of Justice Douglas: A Symposium on Individual Freedom
Robert H. Keller, Jr., editor

A Constitutional History of Habeas Corpus
William F. Duker

The American Codification Movement: A Study of Antebellum Legal Reform
Charles M. Cook

Crime and Punishment in Revolutionary Paris
Antoinette Wills

AMERICAN LEGAL CULTURE, 1908-1940

JOHN W. JOHNSON

CONTRIBUTIONS IN LEGAL STUDIES, NUMBER 16

GREENWOOD PRESS
WESTPORT, CONNECTICUT • LONDON, ENGLAND

Library of Congress Cataloging in Publication Data

Johnson, John W   1946-
    American legal culture, 1908-1940.

    (Contributions in legal studies ; no. 16 ISSN
0147-1074)
        Bibliography: p.
        Includes index.
        1.   Law--United States--History and criticism.
I. Title. II. Series.
KF371.J63   349.73   80-1027
ISBN 0-313-22337-8 (lib. bdg.)

Library of Congress Catalog Card Number: 80-1027
ISBN: 0-313-22337-8
ISSN: 0147-1074

First published in 1981

Greenwood Press
A division of Congressional Information Service, Inc.
88 Post Road West, Westport, Connecticut 06881

Printed in the United States of America

10 9 8 7 6 5 4 3 2 1

To my parents, Bill and Jean Johnson
—for so many reasons

CONTENTS

ACKNOWLEDGMENTS

Anyone who has labored for several years with a manuscript incurs a number of debts, scholarly and otherwise. In my case, the roster of creditors is embarrassingly long and the accounts are large. I am pleased to have the opportunity here to thank those who assisted me in this project, although my gratitude is small recompense for all of the aid I have received.

The following scholars have offered hard-nosed but constructive criticism of my ideas about twentieth-century legal culture: Milton Cantor, Clarke Chambers, James W. Ely, Jr., Robert W. Gordon, Roger K. Newman, Alan Schaffer, Harry N. Scheiber, Frank Sorauf, William M. Wiecek, and Nancy T. Wolfe. I owe special thanks to Milton M. Klein for his incisive review of a prospectus for this book; to Anthony Nimitz for his provocative suggestions about law and information; to Maxwell Bloomfield and Kermit L. Hall for good counsel and general encouragement in this project. My principal obligation, though, is to Paul L. Murphy. As a teacher, advisor, editor, intellectual model, and friend his stamp is on every page of this book.

A grant from the National Endowment for the Humanities permitted me to try out some of the ideas advanced here in a seminar ably directed by C. Herman Pritchett. Sections of this book have been published previously. Chapter 5 is drawn largely from my article "Retreat From the Common Law?: The Grudging Reception of Legislative History by American Appellate Courts in the Early Twentieth Century," 1978 *Detroit College of Law Review* 413. Two other articles were adapted for use here: "Adaptive Jurisprudence: Some Dimensions of Early Twentieth-Century American Legal Culture," 40 *The Historian* 16 (1977), and "Creativity and Adaptation: A Reassessment of American Jurisprudence, 1801-1857 and 1908-1940," vol. 7, no. 4 *Rutgers-Camden Law Journal* 625-54 (1976) copyrighted 1976 by Rutgers School of Law-Camden. I gratefully acknowledge the permission of the editors of these journals to reprint this copyrighted material. I have also received permission to reprint a passage from Samuel Williston's *Life and Law*, pp. 264-265, published by Little, Brown, and Co. (Boston: 1940). My thanks go, in addition, to Betty Barrett for her careful and speedy typing of the final manuscript.

Throughout this project, I was sustained by the love and forebearance of my wife, Deborah, and sons, Matthew and Noah, who knew when to encourage me, distract me, and leave me alone. This book is dedicated to my parents; the dedication speaks for itself.

AMERICAN LEGAL CULTURE, 1908-1940

1
INTRODUCTION

Without question, one of the most dynamic periods in American legal history was the early twentieth century. Between 1908 and 1940, the country's legal culture was significantly altered by a series of occurrences whose impact is still being felt. The early years of the century witnessed the organization of the country's first truly professional bar, the establishment of formal legal education as the norm rather than the exception for American attorneys, and the introduction of the first successful citizen pressure groups in the judicial process. In terms of the substantive law, the early twentieth century saw the waning of common law litigation and, in its place, the rise of statutory law, administrative law, and constitutional law. The period was also distinguished by the flowering of "sociological jurisprudence" and "legal realism," this country's most weighty contributions to the history of Western legal philosophy.

Although recent scholars have not ignored early twentieth-century American legal history,[1] no satisfactory synthesis of the period has been published.[2] American legal historians themselves have generally expressed two main reasons for the dearth of synthetic studies: the period is extraordinarily complex,[3] and its relative recentness denies to historians an adequate temporal perspective.[4] These are legitimate caveats, but they should not cause legal historians to avoid trying to make some overall sense out of the period. Although this book is by no means a thorough-going synthesis of every important facet of legal history in the early twentieth century, it does attempt to examine a few critical aspects of the legal experience in light of what I term a "penchant for information."

What particularly marked the legal history of early twentieth-century United States was a seemingly ubiquitous concern for finding, fashioning, and using new sources of information. Leading figures in the American legal community—appellate judges, prestigious attorneys, and vocal law professors—operated under the assumption that the procurement of proper information was the essential key to an improvement in the state of American law. In the view of informationally oriented legal luminaries of this period, proper information was necessary for fair judicial decision making, meaningful legal training, well-founded legal research, and cogent legal thinking. This assumption was, upon occasion, consciously articulated, but it was more often implicit in the words and actions of the small but influential group of legal actors who guided the course of American law.

The concept of an informational penchant[5] can also be understood as a "paradigm" for the early twentieth-century American legal experience. Leaving aside much of the peculiar gloss that Thomas Kuhn, his followers, and his critics have grafted onto the word "paradigm,"[6] the understanding of the term here is that of a "constellation of beliefs, values, [and] techniques . . . shared by the members of a given community."[7] A penchant for information, then, is treated here as *the* paradigmatic quality of early twentieth-century American legal history. Certainly, other heuristic ways of ordering the swath of America's legal past between 1908 and 1940 may exist, but they pale in the face of the early twentieth-century legal community's lust for information.

From the perspective of the late twentieth century, at a time when the judicial process seems to be reeling from too many forms, too many conflicting authorities, too many pages of trial records, too many computer printouts—in short, from what Alvin Toffler has called "information overload"[8]—it is illuminating to ponder the condition of a past age in which legal actors, fearful of inadequate data, were consumed by the need to discover, compile, present, or use myriad sources of information. This study seeks to isolate and analyze the crucial dimensions of this informational paradigm in early twentieth-century American legal culture.

Some books naturally introduce themselves; some require a few preliminary comments. I suspect that the latter is the case here. First of all, since this book purports to offer a synthetic perspective for the study of a historical period, much of the research has been drawn from secondary sources. Because some excellent work has been done on early twentieth century legal history, it would have been foolish and certainly presumptuous to ignore the pertinent published sources. Where I have relied upon the ideas or research of others, appropriate scholarly attribution is given. But in a number of cases, I have departed from past views or have advanced some conclusions based upon original research and my own reflection.

Second, while I hope this study may have some value for specialized legal historians, I also have in mind as an audience the general students of American civilization. I heartily support Morton Horwitz's injunction that "every specialist ought to aspire to render his own 'mysterious science' less mysterious."[9] Hence, I have tried to avoid the jargon of the law whenever possible, condemning many technical legal issues to the footnotes. When the problem of multiple audiences could not be resolved with mutual satisfaction to the specialist and the generalist, I chose to throw in my lot with the generalist. One area in which this may be apparent is in my discussion of the holdings of specific court cases. Any work on Anglo-American legal history has to involve some case analysis. However, I have tried to avoid the legal hairsplitting that often results in very narrow statements of the rule of a case. If less discussion of court cases is given here than one might expect in a work on American legal history, it is also because I have consciously tried to heed the advice offered by J. Willard Hurst two decades ago (and reiterated many times since by Hurst and others) that legal historians should begin to investigate other dimensions of a country's legal past rather than merely seek to interpret the reported decisions of its courts.[10] Although reported appellate decisions are not ignored in this study, the emphasis has been placed upon the activities of law writers, lawyers, legal researchers, and law professors. Judges, of course, participated in the penchant for information in the early twentieth century. But courts are, for the most part, reflective institutions: they do not initiate business, and they must depend for their authorities somewhat upon what attorneys suggest to them. So the degree to which appellate courts were informed by extra-legal sources and information is dependent upon and secondary to other dimensions of American legal culture in the period.

Throughout this book, the terms "legal community" and "legal culture" appear with some frequency. The former refers to the most influential members of the American legal profession— prestigious attorneys, appellate judges, and the most published professors at leading law schools. These law-trained individuals functioned as an elite and privileged class within the profession as a whole; they not only took the lead in directing and influencing the course of substantive law in the early twentieth century, but they also established the norms for the conduct of all members of the profession. More importantly, this elite group was responsible for the accession and maintenance of the informational paradigm. The term "legal culture" refers to the cluster of norms, rituals, assumptions, traditions, jargon, and guildlike behavior of the American legal community.[11]

Finally, a few words about the organization of this study are in order. Following this introduction, Chapter 2 offers a brief glance at the "preinformational" nineteenth-century legal culture. Chapters 3 through 7 examine selected components of the penchant for information between 1908 and 1940. Even though these five chapters follow a roughly chronological sequence, numerous overlappings and interconnections are inevitable. Without slighting the historical complexity of the legal experience in the early twentieth century, I have tried to examine in separate chapters the most important aspects of the penchant for information. This choice has meant that some matters frequently discussed by past legal scholars under a single rubric have been considered here under discrete headings. For example, I have chosen to discuss legal realism in chapter 7, after having explored in chapter 6 the 1925 to 1935 movement in law schools to integrate the social sciences and case analysis. Obviously, realism and the "ferment" in legal education were related, but for purposes of clarity, they are discussed separately here. The final chapter, chapter 8, notes the paradox of American legal culture since World War II: increasing data but a declining faith in information.

Notes

1. Taking only work published in the 1970s, the range and quality of writings on early twentieth-century legal history is impressive. Comprehensive treatments of leading early twentieth-century legal figures include: William O. Douglas, *Go East, Young Man: The Early Years* (New York, 1974); Peggy Lamson, *Roger Baldwin: Founder of the American Civil Liberties Union* (Boston, 1976); William Twining, *Karl Llewellyn and the Realist Movement* (London, 1973); Melvin I. Urofsky, *A Mind of One Piece: Brandeis and American Reform* (New York, 1971); and David Wigdor, *Roscoe Pound: Philosopher of Law* (Westport, Conn., 1974). Two excellent studies of important early twentieth-century constitutional issues are Paul L. Murphy, *The Meaning of Freedom of Speech: First Amendment Freedoms from Wilson to FDR* (Westport, Conn., 1972); and Clement Vose, *Constitutional Change: Amendment Politics and Supreme Court Litigation Since 1900* (Lexington, Mass., 1972). The 1970s also witnessed the publication of scathing indictments of American legal education and the legal profession; two such efforts give particular attention to the early twentieth century: Jerold S. Auerbach, *Unequal Justice: Lawyers and Social Change in Modern America* (New York, 1976); and Robert Stevens, "Two Cheers for 1870: The American Law School," 5 *Perspectives in American History* 405 (1971). Finally, one scholar, G. Edward White, has written a series of important articles in various law reviews on early twentieth-century American jurisprudence; these articles have been collected and republished in White's *Patterns of American Legal Thought* (Indianapolis, 1978). See also White's biographical sketches of early twentieth-century judges in *The American Judicial Tradition: Profiles of Leading American Judges* (New York, 1976), pp. 129-291. Given this bonanza of recent legal history offerings, it is no wonder that a leading student of legal historiography has referred to the last few years as witnessing a "great revival" of American legal history. See Robert W. Gordon, "Introduction: J. Willard Hurst and the Common Law Tradition of American Legal Historiography," 10 *Law and Society Review* 9, 12 (1975).

2. The best general survey of American legal history, Lawrence M. Friedman's *A History of American Law* (New York, 1973), treats the post-1900 period only in a twenty-nine page epilogue. Bernard Schwartz' *The Law in America: A History* (New York, 1974) provides more expansive coverage of the early twentieth century than does Friedman's text; however, Schwartz's volume does not offer a very satisfactory framework for the dimensions of legal culture discussed and fails to relate legal changes to general social concerns. The glimmering of a synthesis of early twentieth-century legal history is Grant Gilmore, *The Ages of American Law* (New Haven, 1977), pp. 68-98. But like Friedman's epilogue, Gilmore's chapter on twentieth-century American law is sketchy. Also, curiously, Gilmore himself refuses to take American legal history seriously as a "separate category of legal writing." See Gilmore, pp. 145-146, note 6.

3. See Friedman, p. 567.

4. Ibid., p. 567. See also G. Edward White, "Some Observations on a Course in Legal History," 23 *Journal of Legal Education* 440 (1971); and White, "Some Problems in an Interdisciplinary Approach to Legal History," 1 *Journal of Interdisciplinary History* 491 (1971).

5. In a previous article, I suggested another synthetic framework for early twentieth-century American legal culture. See John W. Johnson, "Adaptive Jurisprudence: Some Dimensions of Early Twentieth Century American Legal Culture," 40 *The Historian* 16 (1977). The criticisms of colleagues and my own reflection have led me to doubt the wisdom of this earlier synthetic approach; the notion of a penchant for information now strikes me as much to be preferred over the synthesis posited in my 1977 article.

6. See Thomas S. Kuhn, *The Structure of Scientific Revolutions* (Chicago, 1970); and Imre Lakatos and Alan Musgrave, eds., *Criticism and the Growth of Knowledge* (New York, 1970).

7. Thomas S. Kuhn, "Postscript—1969," in *The Structure of Scientific Revolutions*, p. 175. See also David A. Hollinger, "T.S. Kuhn's Theory of Science and Its Implications for History," 78 *American Historical Review* 370 (1973).

8. Alvin Toffler, *Future Shock* (New York, 1970), pp. 305ff.

9. Morton J. Horwitz, *The Transformation of American Law, 1780-1860* (Cambridge, Mass., 1977), xi.

10. J. Willard Hurst, "The Law in United States History," 104 *Proceedings of the American Philosophical Society* 518, 521-522 (1960). See also Lawrence M. Friedman, "Some Problems and Possibilities of American Legal History," in Herbert J. Bass, ed., *The State of American History* (Chicago, 1970), pp. 9-10; Byron R. White, "Introduction," 5

Perspectives in American History v, vi-vii (1971); Gordon, "Introduction: J. Willard Hurst and the Common Law Tradition in American Legal Historiography," 44-55; and White, *Patterns of American Legal Thought*, xvii-xix. Volume 5 of *Perspectives in American History* was devoted exclusively to essays on American legal history. Justice Byron White, in his "Introduction" to the volume, recalled Hurst's 1960 plea for legal historians to devote more research efforts to noncourt aspects of legal culture; White then pointed out that only three of the ten essayists in the volume "put primary emphasis on the courts." White, "Introduction," v.

11. A thoughtful discussion of American "legal culture" is included in Herbert Jacob, *Justice in America: Courts, Lawyers, and the Judicial Process*, 2nd ed. (Boston, 1972), pp. 13-17, 43-74.

2
AMERICAN LEGAL CULTURE IN THE PRE-INFORMATIONAL AGE

During the nineteenth century, the American legal system was almost wholly dominated by the judicially administered common law. Appellate judges determined the substance and direction of legal doctrine in grandiloquently written opinions. Although the austere men on the state and federal benches were certainly influenced by everyday events and the currents of opinion, they were loath to admit it.

Even the most cursory glance at leading nineteenth-century American appellate court opinions reveals a somewhat typical pattern of decision making. At the beginning of the opinion, the judge or justice would note the bare facts of the case at bar, next he would announce which legal principle governed the case, and then, in a verbose and dilatory fashion, he would apply the previously articulated principle to the facts and obtain a seemingly inevitable conclusion or legal resolution. Twentieth-century scholars have termed this process the *Grand Style*[1] or *Mechanical Jurisprudence*.[2] What is particularly interesting is that this type of decision making frequently took place with scant reference to outside information or authorities, occasionally even without reference to judicial precedents.

The Judicial Fiat

John Marshall, the Chief Justice of the United States from 1801 to 1835, frequently wrote opinions for the Supreme Court that were predicated upon "legal principles" of his own design. A good example of this is his famous decision in *Fletcher* v. *Peck*.[3] The case concerned a monumental Georgia land fraud from the late eighteenth century. During the 1795 legislative session, a group of land speculators bribed most of the members of the Georgia state legislature so their syndicate would be granted millions of acres of land west of the Yazoo River, what is now a large portion of the states of Alabama and Mississippi. One writer claimed that this may have been the "greatest real estate deal in history."[4] The legislature followed the wishes of the speculators and made the grant, but the so-called "Yazoo Land fraud" was later exposed and most of the corrupt legislators were voted out of office at the first opportunity. A new legislature, composed of fresh faces, voted to revoke the fraudulent grant. However, before the new legislature acted to rescind the fraudulent grant, the original grantees had sold large portions of the Yazoo lands to other speculators who later claimed no knowledge of the first fraudulent grant. For years the status of the Yazoo lands was the subject of Congressional debate and judicial hearings. In 1810 the case reached the U.S. Supreme Court and gave rise to one of Chief Justice Marshall's most important opinions.[5]

Marshall held for the Court that the Contract Clause of the U.S. Constitution, Article I, Section 10 ("No State shall . . . pass any . . . law impairing the obligation of contracts . . ."), forbade the annulment of any state grants, even fraudulent ones. With only a passing allusion to an unspecified section of Sir William Blackstone's famous treatise, *Commentaries on the Laws of England*,[6] Marshall asserted that state grants were contracts.[7] Furthermore, without a shred of evidence and in direct contradiction to the expressed wishes of the framers of the Constitution,[8] he claimed that the Contract Clause was meant to restrain states from impairing legislative grants as well as contracts entered into by two or more private parties. Besides relying upon this bogus rationale for the Contract Clause, Marshall claimed that "general principles which are common to our free institutions"[9] determined the Court's course of action. Marshall never did explain clearly or specifically what those principles were. One scholar has referred to Marshall's reasoning in *Fletcher* v. *Peck* as a prime example of the "judicial fiat," that is, the issuance of a decision having as its linchpin a flat, unsupported assertion about history or law.[10]

These comments on Marshall's majority opinion in the Yazoo land fraud case are not meant to criticize the Chief Justice's decision-making prowess. To the contrary, Marshall's opinion in *Fletcher* v. *Peck* was one of the most important foundation stones for the construction of viable judicial power in the new republic. In retrospect, this is one of Marshall's more fortuitous decisions. It is, however, an instance in which Marshall did not permit facts or history or any threatening information to come between himself and the principle he was enunciating. Other examples of Marshall's unwillingness to provide an informed basis for his most important decisions can be cited.

In *McCulloch* v. *Maryland*,[11] the 1819 case that established a basis for greatly expanded Congressional power, Marshall concluded that the chartering of a national bank was authorized by the Necessary and Proper Clause of the Constitution and by the Constitutional Convention itself, despite evidence from the *Journal of the Proceedings of the Convention*, cited by attorneys arguing the case, that revealed the Convention had explicitly rejected the specific proposal of incorporating a national bank.[12] In a famous dispute between two steamboat companies,[13] the Chief Justice asserted—again without any documentary proof—that the Constitutional Convention of 1787 understood "commerce" to include navigation,[14] thus establishing the Commerce Clause as a viable and potentially expansive constitutional tool. Time and again, Marshall alluded to matters relating to the Constitutional Convention or its historical ambience, but on virtually every occasion he preferred to trust his own memory rather than to consult any sources.[15]

Other famous Supreme Court decisions of the nineteenth century were predicated upon naked judicial fiats.[16] In *Hepburn* v. *Griswold* (the so-called First Legal Tender Case),[17] Chief Justice Chase advanced the undocumented assertion that greenback paper money was forbidden by the Contract Clause of the Federal Constitution. Similarly, in Justice Miller's majority opinion in the *Slaughter-house Cases*,[18] a highly controversial theory of the Fourteenth Amendment was advanced without any authoritative foundation. Finally, in *Plessy* v. *Ferguson*,[19] the infamous 1896 case that grafted the "separate but equal" racial doctrine onto the Fourteenth Amendment, the Court's majority again employed the judicial fiat. Although much of the Court's rhetoric in the *Plessy* case was derived from the swirling currents of social Darwinism so prevalent at the end of the century,[20] references to the writings of William Graham Sumner and Herbert Spencer were absent.

Moving from the Federal Supreme Court to state appellate courts in the nineteenth century, the same predisposition to the judicial fiat is apparent. This is borne out by two famous cases involving railroad accidents in the early 1840s decided by the highest courts of South Carolina and Massachusetts: *Murray* v. *South Carolina Railroad Co.*, decided by the South Carolina Court of Errors in 1841,[21] and *Farwell* v. *Boston & Worcester Railroad Corporation*, handed down by the Supreme Judicial Court of Massachusetts in 1842.[22] These were the country's first appellate cases promulgating the so-called "fellow servant rule" of tort liability, that is, an employee has no cause of action against his employer for an injury caused by the negligence of another employee of the same company.[23]

The fellow servant rule, which had its real origin in an English case, *Priestly* v. *Fowler*, decided a few years before the two American cases,[24] was conceived as an exception to the traditional common law doctrine of *respondeat superior*, namely, that a master can be held liable for the actions of his servants or agents. The English case involved a butcher who was being sued by an employee whose thigh had been fractured when the butcher's van in which he was riding had broken down. It seemed that the van had been carelessly overloaded by another employee of the butcher. The English jurist who authored the decision, Lord Abinger, concluded that shielding the employer from liability in a case such as this was justified for the protection of the master himself from suits stemming from employee carelessness. A contrary ruling, he argued, would carry a master's liability to an alarming extent:

The footman . . . may have an action against his master for a defect in the carriage, owing to the negligence of the coachmaker, . . . the master . . . would be liable to the servant for the negligence of the chambermaid, for putting him into a damp bed. . . .[25]

These and other examples cited by Abinger suggest that this distinguished English jurist was particularly worried about the unsettling impact on a master's household should a "fellow servant rule" not prevail. His concern for the servant was, at best, gratuitous: he submitted that the principle he enunciated would be in the best interests of employees who, henceforth, would be encouraged to exercise caution as well as diligence in the service of their employers.[26]

The South Carolina and Massachusetts cases, although they concerned a type of employment different from that in the English case, *Priestly* v. *Fowler*, were decided in a manner consistent with the English holding. The English case involved a small-town business that was, apparently, the extension of a household; the two American cases involved railroading, an enterprise in which the risks and the likelihood of injuries were much greater than in the small-town butcher's business. Moreover, in the Massachusetts case, the injured employee, a train engineer, and his careless "fellow servant," a switchman, worked in separate divisions of the railroad. The action was occasioned by the switchman's error, which caused the train that the engineer was in to be jolted from the track. The engineer sustained a severed hand. Because of the technical and separate natures of their duties, the engineer had no way of protecting himself from any negligence of the switchman.

The Massachusetts engineer's injury was by no means an unusual occurrence for railroading in the early industrial age. The newly developed steam-powered locomotives and their accouterments, although definitely benefiting the settlement and commerce of the nation, gave rise to hundreds of deaths and hundreds of thousands of serious injuries in the last half of the nineteenth century. The courts rendering their judgments in the *Murray* and *Farwell* cases could not, of course, anticipate the tremendous growth and importance of railroads to America. Nor could the courts have been expected to predict the spate of serious injuries that would be linked to railroading from the Civil War to 1900. What is crucial is that the majorities of the *Murray* and *Farwell* courts, in promulgating the fellow servant rule in America, ignored the special dangers inherent to railroading and industrial concerns generally. Only Justice John Belton O'Neall, dissenting in the South Carolina case, thought it was material that the injury involved railroading, and he made very little of the point.[27]

By the beginning of the Civil War, the fellow servant rule had become virtually part of the national common law. In 1861 the highest court of Wisconsin favorably received the fellow servant doctrine, noting that it had been "sustained by almost unanimous judgments of all the courts both of England and this country."[28] Although it is likely that most of the fellow servant cases that reached state appellate courts in the last half of the nineteenth century involved railroad accidents,[29] the pattern established in the *Murray* and *Farwell* cases of not inquiring into the special dangers of railroading was almost universally maintained.

The fellow servant rule, as applied generally by the courts to various occupations, had two important consequences. First, together with the nineteenth-century doctrine of "assumption of risk" ("that a worker in accepting a job contracts for or 'assumes' the risks inherent in the occupation") and "contributory negligence" ("that an injured employee is barred from suing his employer for an injury if the employee was partly responsible for the injury"), the fellow servant rule placed the burden of a worker's physical welfare squarely upon his own shoulders. In conjunction, these doctrines relieved business (and, of course, government) of virtually any responsibility for industrial accidents. Hence, the working poor were made to pay for the less attractive consequences of industrialization, but the businessman was not forced to cut into his growing profits to indemnify injured workers.[30]

Second, the fellow servant rule made it unnecessary for appellate courts to inquire into the specific hazards of railroading and other dangerous industrial enterprises. During the late nineteenth century, when the fellow servant rule was applied uniformly to any number of businesses and industries, a court did not need to attempt to inform itself about the peculiar conditions or hazards of a specific operation. In the early twentieth century, however,

governmental bureaus and private bodies began to assemble data
on the hazards attending certain industries. For example, in 1910
Interstate Commerce Commission statistics revealed that railroad
accidents occurred at a rate of 2.5 per one hundred railroad employees in the year 1889; by 1906 the rate had doubled to 5.0
accidents per one hundred employees.[31]

Why did the compilations of statistics relating to railroad accidents not begin until the early twentieth century? The existence of
the fellow servant rule is part of the answer. When the fellow
servant rule was applied in a Procrustean fashion to all
industries, it was not necessary from the point of view of a reformer to attempt to inform legislatures or courts of the types or degrees
of hazards of selected industries. However, when the fellow servant
rule began to lose its preeminent place in tort law around the turn
of the century, the appellate judiciary became especially interested
in information on accident rates in different industries.

The fellow servant rule was weakened by a combination of
factors, and the reasons for its decline are numerous and complex.
The sheer number and cost of industrial accidents in the late
nineteenth century not only alarmed the poor but also troubled a
few vocal members of the legal community who agitated for
reform. Judges, not comfortable with the arbitrariness of the
fellow servant rule, fashioned a myriad of exceptions. The development of the contingent fee system of litigation around 1900 made it
worthwhile for hundreds of attorneys to take the cases of poor
workers, thus flooding the courts with employers' liability cases.
State legislatures, in response to reform groups such as the Grang-
ers, began to enact laws about 1870 that mitigated and occasionally
abrogated the fellow servant rule. Finally, in 1908 the federal
government passed the Federal Employers' Liability Act,[32] which
had, as one of its provisions, the abolition of the fellow servant
rule for railroading.

With the post-1900 renunciation of the fellow servant rule, it is
not surprising that government commissions and private bodies
began to compile statistics on industrial accidents and that courts
began to avail themselves of this information. (The early twentieth-
century compilation of statistics on industrial hazards is taken up
in the next chapter.) But for most of the late nineteenth century,

the fellow servant rule coincided with a reluctance on the part of state appellate judges to seek out possibly instructive information on industrial accidents. This serves as another extended example of the anti-informational cast of nineteenth-century legal culture.

The Heavy Hand of the Common Law

Why did nineteenth-century legal actors stick to the authority of previous court decisions, intermixed with an occasional judicial fiat? An understanding of why nineteenth-century appellate judges and other participants in the American judicial process of the period seldom ventured beyond common law authority places in stark relief some of the twentieth-century practices discussed in subsequent chapters.

First, as mentioned previously, the so-called Grand Style of judicial opinion writing militated against the urge to wander far from the common law. The great judges of the early republic seemed to pride themselves on their ability to milk a single common law precedent for all it was worth. Occasionally, as was the case with Marshall, if a common law precedent did not exist to serve as an authority for the principle that the judge wanted to discuss, he simply announced it *ex cathedra* in the form of a judicial fiat. The opinion of a judge or justice writing in the Grand Style seemed to exude a spirit of virtual omniscience. In an opinion like *Gibbons* v. *Ogden*, in which the importance of the Commerce Clause of the Federal Constitution was trumpeted, John Marshall made it appear as if he was articulating some eternal legal postulates that one simply could not question.[33] Likewise, throughout the first half of the nineteenth century, the highest courts of several northeastern states fashioned the law of negligence virtually out of whole cloth and made it into one of the most important legal doctrines in support of American economic growth.[34] One of the central cases in the line of negligence decisions was *Brown* v. *Kendall*,[35] decided by the Supreme Judicial Court of Massachusetts in 1850. The majority opinion in this case was written by Chief Justice Lemuel Shaw, the jurist who also wrote the opinion in the *Farwell* case. Shaw's opinion in *Brown* v. *Kendall* was written with the certitude and boldness typical of the Grand Style at its best. The power and farsightedness of the opinions of the great judges of the early nineteenth century—Marshall, Shaw, Joseph Story, James Kent, and Roger Taney—have drawn high praise from legal historians.[36]

Although the nineteenth-century American legal community generally chose to be guided by the spirit—if not the letter—of the common law, on rare occasions judges of the period permitted what can be termed "extra-legal" authorities to creep into their opinions. For example, *The Federalist*, the remarkable series of apologies for the ratification of the U.S. Constitution written in 1787 and 1788 by James Madison, Alexander Hamilton, and John Jay, has been alluded to on numerous occasions for insight into the intentions of the Founding Fathers. The U.S. Supreme Court cited parts of the Eighty-five separate essays of *The Federalist* in over one the poor. Although he acquired a good measure of financial success classical antiquity were also apparent in the opinions of a few early American appellate judges. George Wythe, Chancellor of the Virginia High Court of Chancery from 1788 to 1801, a judge who was reluctant to cite precedents of any sort, made eighty-five classical allusions in his written opinions, sixty-six of which were tied to specific classical sources such as the *Corpus Iuris Civilis* and the writings of Virgil and Cicero. For Wythe, these classical references were not merely stylistic flourishes; they often were cited as legitimate legal precedents in their own right.[38] On the other hand, even though nineteenth-century appellate judges frequently referred to historical events or the "lessons of history," they generally trusted their memories rather than cited historical documents or secondary accounts of past events.[39] On the whole, "extra-legal" authorities in nineteenth-century appellate court opinions were the exception rather than the rule.[40]

A second reason for the infrequent appearance of extra-legal authorities in nineteenth-century judicial opinions is that judges were bound in—or allowed themselves to be bound in—by certain rules and customs relating to proper judicial documentation. An observation of this state of affairs was made by the noted economist Richard T. Ely. In 1906, in a mildly perturbed letter to his longtime friend, Justice Oliver Wendell Holmes, Ely complained:

I see the U.S. Supreme Court has adopted absolutely and almost word for word my definition of monopoly. . . . The justice [McKenna] uses the quotation marks, saying "to quote another," . . . but does not mention my

Monopolies and Trusts. . . . It took me years to work out this definition. . . . I know that in opinions private authors (except law books) are
seldom mentioned, but is that quite fair? . . . [T]he recognition of my work
would have been very welcome.[41]

Ely might have been relieved to know that, although legal treatises
and other textbooks were frequently cited by English appellate
courts before the nineteenth century, after the Napoleonic Wars the
English courts and some American courts followed the custom of
citing only the works of deceased authors.[42] Even though legal
treatises were probably the most frequently cited "persuasive
authorities" (as opposed to binding common law precedents) by
nineteenth-century appellate courts, only a few treatises were cited
with any regularity: William Blackstone's *Commentaries on the
Laws of England*,[43] Joseph Story's *Commentaries on the Constitution of the United States*,[44] Thomas M. Cooley's *Constitutional
Limitations*,[45] and Christopher Tiedeman's *Treatise on the Limitations of the Police Power*.[46] But aside from the important role the
latter two texts played in the accession of a laissez-faire economic
ideology within the legal community at the end of the nineteenth
century,[47] most treatises followed rather than cut a path for the
case law.

At the trial court level, the complex rules of evidence that pre-
vailed throughout the nineteenth century served to restrict the
judicial cognizance of merely "persuasive" published authorities
such as treatises. A published treatise could not be introduced into
evidence because it was clearly hearsay, because no opportunity
would arise to cross-examine the textbook unless the author were
available for testifying, because such a textbook was not written
under oath, and because information contained in the text might be
based upon knowledge in a field that was only of transitory acceptance.[48] In addition, at both the trial and appellate levels, the
doctrine of "judicial notice" restricted reliance upon textbook
authority. Judicial notice refers to a court's independent acquisition
of information pertinent to the determination of a case.[49] The
nineteenth-century position on the question of if and when it was
permissible for judges to take judicial notice of information
contained in textbooks or treatises was blurred, at best. One
commentator, in submitting that "the cases and statutes [establish-

ing the law of judicial notice] are in cloudy confusion," documented this chaos with a nine and one-half page footnote that cited the conflicting authorities from various jurisdictions.[50]

Another reason why the information that reached the nineteenth-century courts was limited relates to the character of the legal profession of the period. Even if judges had expressed a willingness to pay heed to information outside of the bound volumes of court reports, lawyers and most judges themselves were not prepared to assemble or assess such information. Before the Civil War, few American attorneys or judges received any formal legal education. The typical lawyer of 1835, for example, had a grammar school background and learned his law during a period of apprenticeship, usually two years or less, to a member of his state's bar. Given the scarcity of published books, especially west of the Appalachians, the apprentice lawyer did not benefit from wide reading. If he was fortunate, the man for whom he was serving as an apprentice provided him with a copy of Blackstone's *Commentaries* (or Kent's *Commentaries*). In most cases, this treatise was the sole authoritative discussion of the law that the young man read before he began arguing cases or writing briefs.[51] Given, then, the typical early nineteenth-century lawyer's lack of a liberal education, his probable dearth of any formal legal training, and his isolation from published treatises and other books, it is not surprising that he seldom flavored his briefs and arguments with authorities other than the case law or an occasional allusion to Blackstone. Since almost all nineteenth-century judges grew up and were trained under these conditions, they too tended to be narrowly legalistic in their use of authorities.

Those few nineteenth-century jurists who were capable of sophisticated thought and had a taste for scholarly study were allowed little time to indulge these intellectual passions. Judicial case loads were heavy at both the state and federal levels. To fulfill the obligations to their jurisdictions, virtually all judges of the period were required to travel and hold court in several different locales. This "riding circuit" was time-consuming and enervating. Even U.S. Supreme Court justices were required to ride circuit at least once a term.[52] To this end, a justice was required to travel hundreds of miles a year, usually on horseback. As the physical boundaries of the nation expanded, so did the size of the justices' circuits. Yet members of the Supreme Court were not officially relieved of the burden of riding circuit until the passage of an Act of Congress in 1891[53] that created a middle level of courts in the federal system, the Circuit Courts of Appeal.

The nineteenth-century American legal community's bias against sources of information other than the case law was also related to two significant but very different thrusts within formal legal education. First, the limited budding of formal legal education that had occurred in the years since the American Revolution was severely cut back by the upsurge of an egalitarian spirit in the 1830s and 1840s. In the early years of the nineteenth century, leading eastern universities had begun to provide a welcome home for some of the best of the private law schools that had sprouted since the Revolution. With these unions, the integration of skilled, practical legal training with a liberal university education appeared possible for the first time in American history. In 1823 Harvard University made the demand that students in the Law School be graduates of a four-year college or its equivalent, and in 1829 Harvard appointed the scholarly Joseph Story to its law faculty. Story, more than any other legal figure of the period, was the epitome of the liberally educated yet skilled attorney.[54]

Second, just as Story and Harvard appeared ready to lead formal legal education into a golden era, Jacksonian Democracy took hold. Lawyers, particularly educated lawyers, became objects of suspicion, even scorn, to politicians and the general public. Alexis de Tocqueville's mid-1830s observation that lawyers were America's aristocrats[55] was shared by many Americans. But a rapidly expanding, commercial society could not afford to purge all of its lawyers. So a concerted effort was made to "democratize" the legal profession. States began to slash requirements for admission to the bar. In 1800 fourteen of the nineteen states required a specified period of apprenticeship before admission to the bar; by 1840 only eleven of the thirty states had such a requirement; and by 1860 apprenticeship was required only in nine of the thirty-nine states; only one of these nine was a southern state (South Carolina) and only one was west of the Appalachians (Ohio).[56] Just as apprenticeship was going out of fashion, so was formal legal training. Most aspiring lawyers turned their backs on the newly established university law schools. In 1840 the nation had only 345 students attending its nine university-affiliated law schools. Those few law schools that could afford to keep their doors open reduced their standards and scaled down their curricula until only "practical" courses were offered.[57] Thus, the thirty years before the Civil War saw Story's dream of a liberally educated legal profession fade from view. One definite consequence of this state of affairs was that attorneys who did meet the relatively low standards for admission to the state bars between 1830 and 1860 were not exposed to sources of legal insight beyond the reported case law of their jurisdictions. Jacksonian Democracy, therefore, strengthened the grip of the already heavy hand of the common law on the midnineteenth-century legal community.

After the Civil War, certain changes in pedagogy at the Harvard Law School occurred that are still regarded as among the most important shifts in the history of American legal education. Ironically, although commentators have generally referred to the changes at Harvard in the 1870s as serving to improve or "professionalize" legal instruction,[58] their cumulative effect was to limit the influence of noncommon law authorities and sources of information on the legal community.

In 1869 Charles Eliot, a scientist, was appointed president of Harvard. In the following year, Eliot appointed Christopher Columbus Langdell to the newly created post of dean of the Law School, where he served until 1895. During Langdell's tenure, Harvard reestablished itself as the premier law school in the country. With his appointment, law took its first serious step toward becoming a respectable and rigorous subject of university education. Almost immediately, Langdell proposed that members of his faculty make two changes in their modes of instruction. First, he urged that they abandon the lecture method of instruction whenever possible. They were, instead, encouraged to question the students closely about the substance of their assigned reading. This approach is still euphemistically referred to as "Socratic dialogue." Second, Langdell pushed hard for the adoption of the *case method* as a means of instruction, whereby students were required to read selected appellate court opinions that supposedly contained basic legal principles or rules. The student, assisted by the penetrating questions and caustic comments of his professor, then had to ferret out for himself the essential rules of law. The Socratic and case methods thus served a dual purpose: they aided the student in "discovering" the rules of the law, and they indoctrinated the student in the mode of thinking that Langdell and his faculty thought was necessary for proper legal reasoning.

The Harvard approach spread shortly to other law schools. By World War I, most of the faculty at the leading eastern and midwestern law schools had followed Harvard's lead in adopting Socratic questioning and the case method.[59] Harvard's concept of legal education was emulated, especially in the early years, because it appeared to work well. Langdell believed that the law was a science and could be transmitted to bright and hardworking young men with efficiency and effectiveness. Harvard-educated attorneys graduated with an impressive knowledge of the "black-letter law" (basic legal rules) and a developed ability to apply legal principles to varied factual situations. Their successes in practice, in business, and on the bench were widely envied. Upon appointment as professors and deans at other law schools, they began to spread the gospel.

One of the effects of the case method was to warn judges and attorneys against the possible urge to refer to noncase evidence in their decisions and appellate briefs. Langdell maintained that all of the available materials of the "science" of law were contained in printed books—primarily the reports of appellate court decisions. He believed that the law was a self-sufficient system: its premises were formulated by lawyers, and its growth required only the logical development of the precedents laid down in the reported decisions. Langdell's first casebook on contracts, published in 1871, reflected these attitudes.[60] Years later, in an address to the Law School, Langdell succinctly stated the postulates of his case method: "First, that the law is a science; secondly, that all of the available materials of that science are contained in printed books."[61] Thus, the Langdell-inspired, case-trained lawyer found little need to rest his arguments on noncase materials. Even references to "hornbooks" (legal treatises) were discouraged by the Langdell system.

Besides narrowing the field of vision of the practicing attorneys and attorneys to be, the case method militated against thoughtful legal scholarship. Law professors, at the urging of Langdell and his disciples, spent their time editing casebooks and (less frequently) writing treatises. Yet, of the mountain of legal texts produced in the late nineteenth and early twentieth centuries, few were successful in burrowing beneath the formal surface of the law to get at its actual functioning in society.[62] Oliver Wendell Holmes' *The Common Law*[63] proved to be a rare exception. Scholarly writing on constitutional law, especially, suffered neglect from the law writers trained in the case method. Constitutional law provided none of the order that one found in the law of contracts or the law of trusts and estates. To those of Langdell's persuasion, this meant that constitutional law was less scientific. As a result, the science-prone students, whose legal thinking was forged by the case method, tended to shy away from discussing this anomalous aspect of an otherwise orderly subject. A recently published history of American attitudes toward free speech in the 1920s found "practically no satisfactory judicial discussion" of the free speech clauses of the federal Constitution before 1917.[64] This state of scholarly neglect in the late nineteenth and early twentieth centuries can well be laid at the door of Langdell and his intellectual progeny.

Therefore, although the Langdell thrust in American legal education served to sharpen the students' legal reasoning, it also constricted the intellectual field of vision of the students and faculty, and it limited the range of sources of legal information available to aspiring lawyers and their law professors. In short, Langdell and his reforms served to strengthen the already tight grip of the common law upon late nineteenth-century American legal culture.

Notes

1. Karl Llewellyn, "Remarks on the Theory of Appellate Decision and the Rules or Canons About How Statutes Are to be Construed," 3 *Vanderbilt Law Review* 396 (1950).
2. Roscoe Pound, "Mechanical Jurisprudence," 8 *Columbia Law Review* 605 (1908).

3. 10 U.S. (6 Cranch) 87 (1810).

4. Albert J. Beveridge, quoted in C. Peter Magrath, *Yazoo: Law and Politics in the New Republic* (New York, 1967), p. 7.

5. For an excellent discussion of the Yazoo land fraud and *Fletcher* v. *Peck*, see Magrath, passim.

6. 4 vols. (London, 1765-69). The first American edition of Blackstone's *Commentaries* appeared in 1771-72.

7. *Fletcher* v. *Peck*, at 136-137.

8. James Madison, *Notes of Debates in the Federal Convention of 1787*, Adrienne Koch, ed. (New York, 1969), p. 542. Of course, Madison did not publish his notes of the convention debates until more than thirty years after *Fletcher* v. *Peck*. However, Marshall's knowledge of the proceedings of the convention was intimate; it is likely that he knew his view of the Contract Clause was not shared by Madison and the other drafters of the Constitution. See Marie Carolyn Klinkhamer, "The Use of History in the Supreme Court, 1789-1835," 36 *University of Detroit Law Journal* 553 (1959).

9. *Fletcher* v. *Peck*, at 139.

10. Alfred H. Kelly, "Clio and the Court: An Illicit Love Affair," *The Supreme Court Review* 119, 122-123 (1965).

11. 17 U.S. (4 Wheat.) 316 (1819).

12. Jacobus ten Broek, "Admissibility and Use by the United States Supreme Court of Extrinsic Aids in Constitutional Construction," 26 *California Law Review* 437, 448-449 (1938). See also Madison, pp. 638-639.

13. *Gibbons* v. *Ogden*, 22 U.S. (9 Wheat.) 1 (1824).

14. Ibid., at 188-189.

15. Klinkhamer, "The Use of History in the Supreme Court, 1789-1835," 555, 564-577.

16. See Kelly, "Clio and the Court," 122-125.

17. 75 U.S. (8 Wall.) 603 (1870).

18. 83 U.S. (16 Wall.) 36 (1873).

19. 163 U.S. 537 (1896).

20. See generally Barton J. Bernstein, "*Plessy* v. *Ferguson*: Conservative Sociological Jurisprudence," 48 *Journal of Negro History* 196 (1963).

21. 26 S.C.L. (1 McMul.) 385 (1841).

22. 45 Mass. (4 Met.) 49 (1842).

23. The fellow servant rule has benefited from several thorough discussions by legal historians and other scholars. See esp. Lawrence M. Friedman and Jack Ladinsky, "Social Change and the Law of Industrial Accidents," 67 *Columbia Law Review* 51 (1967); and Carl A. Auerbach, Lloyd K. Garrison, Willard Hurst, and Samuel Mermin, *The Legal Pro-*

cess: An Introduction to Decision-Making by Judicial, Legislative, Executive, and Administrative Agencies (San Francisco, 1961), pp. 12-32, 149-166, et passim.

24. 150 Eng. Rep. 1030 (Exchequer, 1837).

25. Ibid., at 1032.

26. Ibid., 1032ff.

27. 26 S.C.L. (1 McMul.) 385, 390 (1841).

28. *Moseley* v. *Chamberlain*, 18 Wis. 700, 705 (1861).

29. *Wisconsin Bureau of Labor and Industrial Statistics: Thirteenth Biennial Report* (1909), p. 26, quoted in Friedman and Ladinsky, "Social Change and the Law of Industrial Accidents," 60, note 34.

30. Morton J. Horwitz, *The Transformation of American Law, 1780-1860* (Cambridge, Mass., 1977), pp. 99-101, 207-210.

31. *Wisconsin Bureau of Labor and Industrial Statistics: Fourteenth Biennial Report* (1911), p. 99, quoted in Friedman and Ladinsky, "Social Change and the Law of Industrial Accidents," 60, note 34.

32. 35 Stat. 65 (1908).

33. *Gibbons* v. *Ogden*, at 190.

34. Horwitz, pp. 85-101.

35. 6 Cush. 292 (Mass. 1850).

36. See Roscoe Pound, *The Formative Era of American Law* (Boston, 1938), passim; Daniel Boorstin, *The Americans: The National Experience* (New York, 1958), pp. 35ff; Charles Harr, ed., *The Golden Age of American Law* (New York, 1965), passim; Perry Miller, *The Life of the Mind in America: From Revolution to the Civil War* (New York, 1965), pp. 117-155; and Grant Gilmore, *The Ages of American Law* (New Haven, 1977), pp. 19-40. Cf. John W. Johnson, "Creativity and Adaptation: A Reassessment of American Jurisprudence, 1801-1857 and 1908-1940," 7 *Rutgers-Camden Law Journal* 625 (1976).

37. Charles W. Pierson, "*The Federalist* in the Supreme Court," 33 *Yale Law Journal* 728, 734 (1924).

38. Richard J. Hoffman, "Classics in the Courts of the United States, 1790-1800," 22 *American Journal of Legal History* 55, 57-59 (1978).

39. See Klinkhamer, "The Use of History in the Supreme Court, 1789-1835," 565; and ten Broek, "Admissibility and Use by the United States Supreme Court of Extrinsic Aids in Constitutional Construction," 291ff, 308, 445-446, 448.

40. See John W. Johnson, "The Dimensions of Non-Legal Evidence in the American Judicial Process: The United States Supreme Court's Use of Extra-Legal Materials in the Twentieth Century" (Unpublished Ph.D. Dissertation: University of Minnesota, 1974), pp. 10-100.

41. Richard T. Ely to Oliver Wendell Holmes, Jr., October 24, 1906, quoted in Benjamin G. Rader and Barbara K. Rader, "The Ely-Holmes Friendship, 1901-1914," 10 *American Journal of Legal History* 128, 138 (1966).

42. Max Radin, "Sources of Law—New and Old," 1 *Southern California Law Review* 42 (1928).

43. On the use of Blackstone by American lawyers and judges, see George Sharswood, "A Memoir of Sir William Blackstone," in Blackstone, *Commentaries on the Laws of England*, George Chase, ed. (Boston, 1876). See also Daniel J. Boorstin, *The Mysterious Science of the Law* (Cambridge, Mass., 1941), Introduction.

44. (Boston, 1833).

45. The full title of Cooley's volume is *A Treatise on the Constitutional Limitations Which Rest upon the Legislative Powers of the States of the American Union* (Boston, 1868).

46. The full title of Tiedeman's volume is *Treatise on the Limitations of the Police Power in the United States* (St. Louis, 1886).

47. The use of the authority of the treatises by Cooley and Tiedeman in the rise of laissez-faire constitutionalism is discussed in Clyde E. Jacobs, *Law Writers and the Courts: The Influence of Thomas M. Cooley, Christopher G. Tiedeman, and John F. Dillon Upon American Constitutional Law* (Berkeley, 1954); Benjamin R. Twiss, *Lawyers and the Constitution: How Laissez Faire Came to the Supreme Court* (Princeton, 1942); and Arnold M. Paul, *Conservative Crisis and the Rule of Law: Attitudes of Bench and Bar, 1887-1895* (Ithaca, N.Y., 1960).

48. On the use of textbook authority at the trial court level, see Edward W. Cleary, ed., *McCormick's Handbook on the Law of Evidence*, 2nd ed. (St. Paul, Minn., 1972), section 321; and Warren M. Dana, "Admission of Learned Treatises in Evidence," *Wisconsin Law Review* 455, 455-459 (1945). On the problems associated with text authority, particularly from the social sciences, the literature is voluminous; but see esp. Edmond Cahn, "A Dangerous Myth in the School Segregation Cases," 30 *New York University Law Review* 150 (1955).

49. On judicial notice, see Edmund M. Morgan, "Judicial Notice," 57 *Harvard Law Review* 269 (1944); Harold L. Korn, "Law, Fact, and Science in the Courts," 66 *Columbia Law Review* 1080 (1966); Charles T. McCormick, "Judicial Notice," 5 *Vanderbilt Law Review* 296 (1952); and Kenneth Culp Davis, "Judicial Notice," 55 *Columbia Law Review* 945 (1955).

50. John T. McNaughton, "Judicial Notice—Excerpts Relating to the Morgan-Wigmore Controversy," 14 *Vanderbilt Law Review* 779, 795ff (1961).

51. See Sharswood, "A Memoir of Sir William Blackstone"; and Boorstin, pp. 31-61.

52. 1 Stat. 73 (1789).

53. 26 Stat. 826 (1891).

54. Robert Stevens, "Two Cheers for 1870: The American Law School," 5 *Perspectives in American History* 405, 418 (1971).

55. Alexis de Tocqueville, *Democracy in America*, Phillips Bradley, ed. (New York, 1945), I, pp. 288-289.

56. Alfred Z. Reed, *Training for the Public Profession of the Law* (New York, 1921), pp. 86-87.

57. Ibid., p. 140. See also Brainerd Currie, "The Materials of Law Study, Part I," 3 *Journal of Legal Education* 331, 374 (1951); and Stevens, "Two Cheers for 1870," 418-419.

58. See generally Currie, "The Materials of Law Study" and Stevens, "Two Cheers for 1870."

59. A good brief discussion of the case method, as conceived by Langdell, and its spread from Harvard to other law schools can be found in Stevens, "Two Cheers for 1870," 426-441.

60. Christopher C. Langdell, *A Selection of Cases on the Law of Contracts* (Boston, 1871), iv.

61. Quoted in Charles Warren, *History of the Harvard Law School and of Early Legal Conditions in America* (New York, 1908), II, p. 374.

62. James Willard Hurst, *The Growth of American Law: The Law Makers* (Boston, 1950), p. 171.

63. (Boston, 1881).

64. Paul L. Murphy, *The Meaning of Freedom of Speech: First Amendment Freedoms from Wilson to FDR* (Westport, Conn., 1972), pp. 248-249. See also Murphy, *World War I and the Origin of Civil Liberties in the United States* (New York, 1979), pp. 17-19, 133.

3
A REVOLUTION IN LEGAL ANALYSIS: THE STRATEGIC GENIUS OF LOUIS BRANDEIS

On a cold winter afternoon in 1914, Judge William Hitz of the District of Columbia Supreme Court paused to converse with his friend Charles Henry Butler, a distinguished lawyer and the official reporter of U.S. Supreme Court decisions. Both men had just witnessed the oral argument of Louis Brandeis before the U.S. Supreme Court in defense of an Oregon minimum wage statute.[1] Butler, like many members of the Court who had heard Brandeis's appeal, was suspicious and even frightened of the "socialism" that the famous attorney was alleged to espouse. Yet, he admitted to Hitz that no man in the current term of the Court had captured such close attention from the justices as Brandeis had that day.[2]

Brandeis's oral argument in the Oregon minimum-wage case was reminiscent of his famous argument in defense of another Oregon law in the earlier case of *Muller* v. *Oregon*.[3] On January 15, 1908, Brandeis spoke before the Supreme Court in favor of an Oregon statute that limited the hours a woman could work in laundries or other industries within the state. That date marked the beginning of a new era in American legal history, an era dominated by information and one in which the impact of Louis Brandeis was preeminent. No individual more epitomized the penchant for information in early twentieth-century American legal history than did Brandeis, and no individual was more responsible for bringing others to share this fascination for and dependence upon information.

It is tempting to employ a "great man" hypothesis in explaining Brandeis's information-oriented role in the American judicial process.[4] His appellate briefs, his post-1916 Supreme Court opinions, and various judicial practices that he pioneered clearly establish his informational bent as foremost among his contemporaries. However, American law would have evidenced an informational penchant in the early twentieth century even without the example and urgings of Brandeis. In the first decade of the century, a certain informational matrix was becoming evident in the activities and writings of leading members of the American legal community; it would have continued to form without Brandeis, but its texture would have been different and perhaps not as rich. Yet, Brandeis did take the lead in creating the intellectual basis for this important shift in legal culture. His leadership and his example warrant attention before additional dimensions of the informational paradigm can be flushed out.

The Brandeis Brief

More than Brandeis's style in oral argument that so impressed Hitz and Butler, it is the written appellate brief that Brandeis submitted in the *Muller* case[5] that has properly been the subject of so much attention by legal and constitutional scholars.[6] Unlike past appellate arguments that relied upon case precedents, the so-called "Brandeis brief" in the *Muller* case alluded strictly to legal authorities on only 3 of its 113 pages. Most of Brandeis's support for his position was drawn from government labor statistics, reports of factory inspectors, and testimony from psychological, economic, and medical treatises. Sources such as these had rarely been called to the attention of appellate courts before 1908, and never had any attorney drawn so heavily upon such extra-legal authorities in a single brief. Even though much of the story of the birth and influence of the "Brandeis brief" is well known, some of it needs to be retold here to make clear why the Brandeis brief was *the* essential first step in the fashioning of an informational mind-set among the most influential members of the early twentieth-century American legal community.

In 1905 when the U.S. Supreme Court, in the famous case of *Lochner* v. *New York*,[7] overturned a state law limiting the hours men were permitted to work in bakeries, it became obvious to lawyers and social reformers that the Court was unwilling or unable to confront the realities of the prevailing social and economic situation. The *Lochner* majority relied upon the curious "liberty of contract" principle, which, the Court claimed, radiated from the Due Process Clause of the Fourteenth Amendment and "protected" employees from having state legislatures deny their "freedom" to work twelve, fourteen, or even sixteen hours a day. The assumption entertained (or at least tacitly accepted as a rationalization) by the apostles of laissez-faire on the Supreme Court was that the employer and employee operated as equal partners in the labor relationship. Thus, both should be permitted to bargain freely without state interference. However, in reality, the industrial worker of 1905—as any reader of Upton Sinclair's *The Jungle* can testify— was an unequal partner in the "bargain." He had to accept what employment was available, regardless of the conditions imposed or the duties required. He did not contract to work eighty hours a week; he was compelled to do so by the exigencies of his desperate economic straits.

In the *Muller* case, Brandeis was asked to defend a maximum-hours law similar to the one struck down in *Lochner* v. *New York*. However, whereas the New York law related to men working in bakeries, the Oregon statute placed a limit on the hours of work during a week that women could toil in the laundries or factories in the state. Given the composition of the Court in 1908, Brandeis was wise in reasoning that the *Lochner* precedent should not be assaulted frontally. Such a maneuver would undoubtedly have failed, as it had failed in the *Lochner* case itself. Thus, in the short section of his brief headed "Argument,"[8] he acknowledged the points of law established in the 1905 decision. In substance, he maintained that the gloss put on the Fourteenth Amendment by the "liberty of contract" principle was valid. That is, a state could not normally enact legislation restricting hours of labor in industry. However, Brandeis focused upon the exception to this rule, which had also been enunciated in *Lochner*: that the "liberty of contract" is subject to such a reasonable restraint of action as a state may impose in exercise of its "police power" for the protection of "health, safety, morals, and the general welfare."[9]

To demonstrate that the Oregon legislation was reasonable in light of these considerations, Brandeis entrusted his sister-in-law Josephine Goldmark with the task of tracking down and compiling "facts" about the effects of long hours on the "health, safety, morals and general welfare of women" from works published by industry experts. Goldmark was a hardworking and aggressive social reformer and an active member of the National Consumers' League, one of the first reform-oriented pressure groups to attempt to influence judicial decisions. In 1907 she was the chairman of the League's Committee on Legislation. It was principally because of her urgings, backed by the League's leadership, that Brandeis was chosen as counsel for the state of Oregon in defense of its maximum-hours law for women.[10] Hence, the League and Brandeis directly conducted the appeal of the case to the Supreme Court; being able to submit his innovative brief as one of the parties certainly gave it more weight with the Supreme Court than if it had been simply filed as an *amicus curiae*.[11] The fact that the state of Oregon would follow the suggestion of an independent pressure group like the National Consumers' League and relinquish conduct of such an important appeal is testimony either to the influence of the League or the attractiveness of an attorney as skilled and as socially motivated as Louis Brandeis—or both.

By the early twentieth century, Brandeis had achieved an unsurpassed reputation as a staunch supporter of the working class and the poor. Although he acquired a good measure of financial success at the behest of corporate clients, by about 1890 Brandeis had begun the practice of offering his legal talents at little or no cost to reform causes, earning for himself the accolade of "the people's lawyer." In 1897 he spoke up for consumers before a Congressional committee; in 1902 he consulted with Clarence Darrow over the preparation of a brief for a group of mine workers; and during the first decade of the twentieth century, he served as counsel without pay in several Massachusetts public welfare contests. Besides supervising the appeal in the *Muller* case, between 1908 and 1914 Brandeis served without pay as counsel for Illinois, Ohio, and California, defending maximum hours and minimum wage legislation. In 1910

he served gratis as the attorney for *Collier's Weekly* in the Ballinger-
Pinchot conservation dispute, and between 1910 and 1916 he was
the unpaid chairman of the Arbitration Board for New York's
garment workers. In 1912 he joined the Zionist Movement, and
between 1911 and his accession to the Supreme Court in 1916, he
was active in so-called "Progressive politics," often advising the
man who later appointed him to the Court, Woodrow Wilson.
Thus, even if Brandeis had never served a day on the Supreme
Court, he would have had an important place in American legal
and political history.[12]

But in 1908 the possibility of Brandeis's future service on the
Supreme Court was not entertained by even the most radical of
dreamers. What many contemporaries referred to as his "socialist
leanings" were clearly not in line with the dominant thrust of the
laissez-faire-oriented Supreme Court of Chief Justice Melville
Fuller. So in defending the Oregon maximum-hours law in the
Muller case, Brandeis was confronted with a difficult task indeed.
The Fuller Court could not easily be persuaded that any state law
restricting the "freedom of contract" in employment was constitutional. By charging Josephine Goldmark with the task of gathering
"facts" on the hazards of long hours of work on the "health,
safety, morals and general welfare of women," Brandeis hoped to
convince the Court that this Act offered one of those exceptional
cases in which a state had good reason to restrain certain business
practices.

Goldmark, with the blessing of the National Consumers' League,
enlisted a group of ten researchers to find the types of facts Brandeis
had in mind. In ten days, having ravaged the Columbia University
Library, the Astor Library, and the Library of Congress for salient
material, Goldmark returned to Boston with a mountain of statistics and quotations that she and Brandeis molded into the soon-to-
be famous brief.[13] The statements quoted in the final brief were
mined from a broad range of published sources—both domestic
and foreign—and included medical reports, psychological treatises,
reports of factory inspectors, extracts of reports from government
bureaus of statistics, and reports from diverse legislative bodies.
Brandeis was careful to note in his legal argument that the statements in his brief did not necessarily prove with conclusiveness that

long hours of labor in factories and laundries were deleterious to the health, safety, and morals of women. Rather, he claimed they revealed only that *some* evidence existed upon which a legislative body could reasonably justify limitations on the liberty of contract.[14] The quality of the evidence cited, Brandeis admitted, might have been lacking in certain respects, but if a reasonably prudent group of legislators could have been led to accept such findings, the standards set down by the Court in *Lochner* did not permit a judicial veto of the Oregon law. The Court, in the unanimous opinion authored by Justice Brewer, agreed in substance with Brandeis:

The legislation and opinions referred to . . . may not be, technically speaking, authorities, . . . yet they are significant of a widespread belief that woman's physical structure, and the functions she performs in consequence therof, justify special legislation restricting or qualifying the conditions under which she should be permitted to toil. . . . [W]hen a question of fact is debated and debatable, and the extent to which a special constitutional limitation goes is affected by the truth in respect to that fact, a widespread and long continued belief concerning it is worthy of consideration.[15]

Of course, Brandeis may have meant to leave the Court with the impression that his facts were *valid*, although he argued only that they *existed* and that a legislature did not act unreasonably by founding legislation upon them, valid or not. Yet, even Brandeis must have been troubled by the haphazard way in which the evidence had been collected and by the incipient state of knowledge in most of the fields from which the data were gleaned. He admitted as much when he registered his original charge to Goldmark to collect any such printed matter "sufficiently authoritative to pass muster."[16]

What needs to be emphasized about Brandeis's brief in the *Muller* case and other Brandeis briefs based upon its example in the years to follow is that they offered lawyers a way of injecting unprecedented amounts of extra-legal information into the judicial process. Brandeis often spoke of the need for courts to be provided with more facts and more "knowledge." What he really meant was more information, more data. He often seemed to say "knowledge" when he meant "information," as in his famous dissent in *Jay Burns Baking Company* v. *Bryan*, written many years after his first Brandeis brief:

Unless we know the facts on which legislators may have acted we cannot properly decide whether they were . . . unreasonable, arbitrary, or capricious. Knowledge is essential to understanding; and understanding should precede judging. Sometimes, if we would guide by the light of reason, we must let our minds be bold.[17]

Although Brandeis's innovative appellate technique has been justly lauded for its legal utility,[18] the brief in the *Muller* case did not offer very sophisticated social science analysis. Implicit in the mass of data and testimony marshalled by Brandeis and Goldmark for the Oregon appeal are five hypotheses: (1) that women, because they are physiologically different from men, are more liable to injury in an unregulated industrial environment; (2) that long hours of labor tend to endanger the health, safety, and morals of women; (3) that "reasonable" working hours sustain industrial health, improve home life, and help the nation in general; (4) that short workdays promote a variety of economic benefits to businesses and customers; and (5) that the various benefits just noted can accrue only from uniform restrictions on the working day. Most of the data, however, in support of these hypotheses was assembled in an unsystematic fashion. No attempt was made to control or isolate any of the multitude of independent variables affecting health, safety, morals, and the general welfare. Finally, none of the hypotheses was actually tested by Brandeis, Goldmark, or any of the other researchers. Yet, the Brandeis-Goldmark method of classification and assembly of data was no worse than much of that which passed for social science in the period. In fact, one commentator's characterization of Brandeis's *Muller* brief as "nascent social science"[19] is an apt appraisal of the quality of the brief and the research out of which it sprang.

To call the evidence and the method behind the *Muller* brief "nascent social science" is not to denigrate its importance as a legal tool. However, Brandeis was not a path-breaking social scientist, and his brief did not advance the state of knowledge about hours of labor and working conditions. Brandeis cared little about real scientific knowledge; his statements to the contrary, as in the above quotation from the *Jay Burns Baking Co.* case, were founded upon an error in diction, namely, his improper use of the word *knowledge*. Brandeis cared very much, though, about the impact

that mountains of data and information would have upon the
Supreme Court in a maximum-hours case such as *Muller* v. *Oregon.*
The data cited in the *Muller* brief, he argued, did not necessarily
prove any of his hypotheses definitely. But he did believe that the
statistical and testimonial information in the brief tended to illustrate that some information existed regarding the hazards of long
hours of labor on the well-being of working women, and the Oregon legislature could have reasonably relied upon it in framing its
maximum-hours law.

So in retrospect the first Brandeis brief appears innovative in its
approach to legal argumentation, orthodox in its support of substantive legal principles (e.g., the endorsement of the general doctrine of "liberty of contract" from the *Lochner* opinion), and rudi-
mentary in its grasp of social science methodology. But the brilliance
of Brandeis's legal strategy in *Muller* was of such great consequence
that it provided a lever to tilt and eventually topple archaic legal
doctrine; it also survived for a sufficient time to participate in the
legal acknowledgment of a much more sophisticated social science.

Spreading the Brandeis Message

If the submission of the information-laden brief in *Muller* had
been a one-time occurrence, legal scholars would probably regard
it as a curious anomaly. But the brief quickly became a model for
appellate argumentation in cases involving economic legislation.
The National Consumers' League and its attorneys prepared fifteen
such Supreme Court briefs in defense of state labor laws between
1908 and 1936.[20] The brief in *Adkins* v. *Children's Hospital*,[21]
prepared by Felix Frankfurter and the League's Mary Dewson,
ran to over 1,100 pages and cost nearly $7,000 to print.[22] In the
thirties, the National Labor Relations Board (NLRB) created a
special "Division of Economic Research" to conduct industrial
studies to assist its attorneys in assembling economic and statistical
evidence for the presentation of Supreme Court appeals. The first
five cases to reach the Supreme Court from the NLRB were argued
by government attorneys of the Division of Economic Research
armed with statistical information in the form of Brandeis briefs. A
survey of some sixty cases involving "labor activity and labor laws,"
decided by the U.S. Supreme Court during the first four decades of

the twentieth century, provides a limited quantitative measure of the strength of the Brandeis brief. In nineteen of the cases, one party to the suit employed substantial economic data (in effect, Brandeis briefs) and the other party did not. The parties partial to the economic evidence were victorious in sixteen of the nineteen cases.[23]

Assembling a Brandeis brief is no simple task. Capable researchers are needed, and thousands of dollars are needed to defray publication costs. Brandeis and the emulators of his technique would not likely have been able to produce prodigiously detailed tomes without the assistance of public-spirited interest groups and wealthy individuals. The National Consumers' League underwrote the cost for the preparation of the *Muller* brief. The cost of printing all of the National Consumers' League appellate briefs before 1935, including the 1,138 page brief in the 1923 *Adkins* case, was paid entirely by the philanthropist Mrs. Willard Straight. In 1909 the Russell Sage Foundation awarded the League $2,500 to be used to survey the scholarly literature on the relationship between hours of labor and fatigue. The fruits of this study quickly found their way into the League's brief in *Ritchie* v. *Wayman*,[24] a state supreme court case in which the Illinois ten-hour law for women was ultimately upheld—perhaps due to the quality of the League's brief.

Three years after the Illinois victory, again with the support of the Russell Sage Foundation, the League published a nine hundred-page synthesis of statistics and testimony on the effects of long hours of labor in industry, titled *Fatigue and Efficiency*.[25] Much of the material incorporated in this volume had appeared in the four earlier National Consumers' League briefs. In turn, this mammoth compendium was relied upon in the League's preparation of appellate briefs during the next twenty-five years.

Besides assembling and printing Brandeis briefs, the National Consumers' League went to great lengths to publicize the content and judicial significance of the information-packed briefs it turned out. The League believed that copies of Brandeis briefs should exist not only for the perusal of lawyers but also for examination by the country's future leaders. Hence, the brief that was prepared for the appeal in *Bunting* v. *Oregon*[26] was distributed at no cost to hundreds of law schools, colleges, libraries, and important individual opinion leaders. The League also issued annual reports, flyers, and leaflets telling of its activities. In addition, it reprinted and distributed scholarly articles supportive of labor legislation. In 1925, with the assistance of another foundation, the League published a collection of articles on the *Adkins* case, titled *The Supreme Court and Minimum Wage Legislation.*[27] Brandeis's genius in conceiving the design for the massively detailed appellate briefs would never have been physically manifested had it not been for the money provided by wealthy individuals and foundations and the enthusiastic labor of the National Consumers' League.

After 1937 economically oriented Brandeis briefs were rarely submitted to the appellate courts. It was in that year that the U.S. Supreme Court sustained a Washington minimum-wage statute in the case of *West Coast Hotel Co.* v. *Parrish.*[28] In upholding this law, the Court's majority alerted the legal profession that it would no longer act as a check upon Congress and state legislatures in matters relating to the reasonableness of legislation regulating the economy. It also made unnecessary the presentation of economically oriented Brandeis briefs. Since economic legislation was, from that point forward, presumed to be constitutional, the defenders of laws establishing maximum hours, minimum wages, codes of industrial behavior, and other economic structures no longer needed to file voluminous briefs. It was no longer necessary to present page upon page of expert testimony and statistical information to convince appellate courts that some evidence existed that might have justified a reasonable legislature to act as it did. With the *Parrish* decision, the Court seemed to give a virtual carte blanche to the legislative prerogative over economic matters.

The *Parrish* result was obtained by the migration of Chief Justice Hughes and Associate Justice Roberts from the ranks of those skeptical of any government regulation of the economy to the so-called liberal position on the Court, which was tolerant of virtually any governmental tinkering with the economy that did not delegate too much regulatory power to big business. This reorientation in the thinking of Hughes and Roberts has been referred to as "the switch in time that saved nine," because it obviated the need for President Franklin Roosevelt to pursue his ill-advised, Court-packing plan that, if passed by Congress, would have allowed the President to appoint as many as six "liberal" justices to the Court.[29] In effect, the Supreme Court in the *Parrish* case was endorsing the position so eloquently advocated by Justice Holmes in his famous *Lochner* dissent,[30] namely, that courts should not sit as super-legislatures but should permit the people's representatives wide latitude in the enactment of economic legislation. Perhaps if Holmes' view had carried the Court in 1905, the need for Brandeis briefs would never have presented itself, and the course of early twentieth-century American legal history would have significantly altered.[31]

The Brandeis Opinion

Although Justice Brewer, in delivering the majority opinion in the *Muller* case, accepted Brandeis's contention that a court should take judicial cognizance of facts bearing on the permissible extents of constitutional limitations, he did not want to take the further step of granting Brandeis's sources legitimacy as constitutional authorities. In his view, reports of government bureaus, statements of factory inspectors, and quotations from medical studies "were not, technically speaking, authorities."[32] Thus, none of Brandeis's atypical sources was mentioned in the body of the majority opinion. The only reference to them was a short "annotation," alluding merely to the general character of the sources in Brandeis's brief; the only specific authority cited in the annotation was an undocumented statement of an "inspector from Hanover."[33]

The first extensive use of Brandeis-style authorities by a Supreme Court Justice did not come until 1917 in the case of *Adams* v. *Tanner*.[34] Not surprisingly, the justice initiating the practice was none other than the newly appointed Louis D. Brandeis. In this case, the Court was faced with a test of the constitutionality of a Washington statute, dubbed the "Employment Agency Law." The law prohibited employment agencies from operating in the state and exacting fees for finding jobs from hopeful employees. In the majority opinion of Justice McReynolds, the Court held that although a state may regulate the operation of employment agencies, it may not constitutionally prohibit their operation. Such a prohibition, McReynolds argued, restricted the "liberty of contract" of employment agencies that was said to be guaranteed by the Due Process Clause of the Fourteenth Amendment.

To this holding and its rationale, Brandeis vigorously dissented.[35] In a detailed nineteen-page opinion, Brandeis chided the Court majority for its unwillingness to look behind the statute to inquire into the basis for the law. Drawing upon a range of source material reminiscent of that encompassed by his brief in the *Muller* case—including reports of the Washington Bureau of Labor, the U.S. Bureau of Labor *Bulletin*, Congressional hearings and testimony, the *Political Science Quarterly*, several texts on labor laws, the *American Labor Legislation Review*, and *Survey* magazine—he submitted that substantial information existed that the Washington legislature could easily have taken into account when it was drafting the law. The authorities Brandeis cited revealed in detail how employment agencies in recent Washington history had literally extorted money from destitute workers, providing them, at best, with short-term, and low-paying jobs; in the extreme, the agencies acted as arms of large corporations, shanghaiing ignorant men to distant locations to labor under primitive conditions, continually subject to brutal discipline. Given these facts, Brandeis submitted that the state of Washington had a reasonable basis for enacting the statute. His thinking on this count paralleled the justification for his earlier data-filled briefs:

. . . Whether a measure relating to the public welfare is arbitrary or un-reasonable, whether it has no substantial relation to the end proposed is obviously not to be determined by assumptions or by *a priori* reasoning. . . . It is necessary to enquire therefore: What was the evil which the people of Washington sought to correct? Why was the particular remedy embodied in the statute adopted? And, incidentally, what has been the experience, if any, of other states or countries in this connection? . . . The sole purpose of the enquiries is to enable this court to decide, whether in view of the facts, actual or possible, the action of the state of Washington was so clearly arbitrary or so unreasonable, that it could not be taken. . . .[36]

Most of Brandeis's information-packed opinions issued while serving on the Supreme Court were in dissent. These dissents were generally sparked by the Court majority's arbitrary overruling of regulatory state laws. A majority that was unwilling to presume the constitutionality of state laws dealing with hours, wages, or conditions of labor often launched Brandeis into a lengthy and detailed

defense of such laws.[37] In *Truax* v. *Corrigan*,[38] a case involving the
constitutionality of an Arizona anti-injunction law, Brandeis offered this rationale for his detailed, highly documented dissent:

> Whether a law enacted in the exercise of the police power is justly subject to
> the charge of being unreasonable or arbitrary, can ordinarily be determined
> only by a consideration of the contemporary conditions, social, industrial
> and political, of the community. . . . Resort to such facts is necessary . . . in
> order to appreciate the evils sought to be remedied and the possible effects
> of the remedy proposed.[39]

Yet, when Brandeis authored majority opinions upholding the
constitutionality of regulatory economic statutes, he seldom resort-
ed to massive barrages of statistics and testimony. In such cases, he
apparently believed the constitutional presumption for economic
regulations was a sufficient rationale in and of itself to allow appellate courts to uphold such laws.[40]

Although Brandeis's novel briefs had helped him achieve a national reputation within the legal profession while still an attorney,
his elevation to the Supreme Court made him even more visible to
the country's intellectuals and opinion leaders. Uneasy feelings
about his reputed radical views had surfaced immediately after the
announcement of his appointment by President Wilson in early
1916. A financial reporter for the *New York Times* claimed that
Wall Street's groaning in response to the prospect of Brandeis on
the Supreme Court was "like the Echo of a great national disaster."
Former President William Howard Taft, a man who valued his
own later appointment to the High Court as more of an honor than
his election to the presidency, received the news of Brandeis's appointment with "a fearful shock," claiming that Brandeis was "a
muckraker, an emotionalist for his own purpose, a socialist, . . .a
man who has . . . much power for evil." Yet, many critics of big
business were in agreement with Attorney General T.W. Gregory's
assessment of Brandeis as "the greatest lawyer in the United States."[41]
The debate over the fitness of Brandeis to sit on the Court continued through a stormy Senate confirmation hearing, ending over
five months after the announcement of the appointment with the
acceptance of Brandeis as an Associate Justice. Strangely, perhaps,

given the virulent antisemitism within the legal profession during the World War I period,[42] Brandeis's religion came in for less criticism than that of his views on business and government.[43]

As a result of all of the turmoil that was associated with Brandeis's nomination, it is not surprising that so much attention was paid by the legal community to the early opinions of the new justice. After all, many Court watchers were curious to see whether Wall Street's fears about Brandeis would be confirmed or denied. The newest member of the Court was well aware of the interest in his views and, consequently, may have tried especially hard in his early opinions to speak to his curious audience. Brandeis took advantage of this situation and, as his principal biographer has suggested, used his early dissenting opinions as educational vehicles.[44] With prominent members of the legal and business communities as his pupils, Brandeis frequently wrote his lectures on social justice into the court reports. Quite often those "lectures" were documented by literature never before cited in Supreme Court opinions: law reviews, trade and professional journals, government reports, and periodicals as diverse as *The Nation* and *Nation's Business*. He refused to rest his opinions upon abstract concepts or vague constitutional theory. As one commentator suggested, Brandeis cleaved to a "jurisprudence of facts" rather than a "jurisprudence of concepts."[45] Brandeis's recitation from these "extra-legal" sources served to bring out information that the new justice believed was relevant to proper appellate decision making.

Probably, Brandeis's notable dissent in *Adams* v. *Tanner* drew as much comment as any of his opinions issued in his first few terms on the Court. Generally, the comment was favorable. For example, a *Yale Law Journal* "Note" approved the dissenting view, observing that the opinion was "remarkable for its modern method of approach and comprehensive marshalling of social data."[46] Also, in reference to the same opinion, Interstate Commerce Commissioner J.S. Harlan wrote to the new justice: "I cannot refrain from telling you what a splendid document it seems to me to be. . . . It cannot be doubted that the conclusions you have reached must in the end prevail."[47] Although opinions of the ilk of the dissent in *Adams* v. *Tanner* may have been heartening to social reformers and liberals in the law schools, they met with little sympathy from Brandeis's Supreme Court colleagues. For instance,

Brandeis frequently alluded to information contained in law review articles. Yet, Brandeis had been a member of the High Court for almost ten years before another justice condescended to cite law review authority in the course of an opinion.[48] In the main, the extensive citation of information from extra-legal sources that Brandeis had introduced in his *Adams* dissent was not mimicked by other justices until the ascendancy of Franklin Roosevelt's appointees to the Court in the late 1930s.[49]

The intransigency of American legal culture in the half dozen years after World War I militated against the writing of judicial opinions laced with statistics, information from government reports, and quotations from law reviews. Brandeis's lone advocacy of a new style of opinion writing was a bit intemperate even for the most tolerant of the legal giants of the period. Although Justices Holmes and Clarke praised Brandeis's dissent in *Adams* v. *Tanner*,[50] they were loath to search out such bastions of information and rely upon them in their own opinions. Shortly after Brandeis began delivering his information-packed dissenting opinions, the distinguished British economist Harold Laski wrote to his old friend Justice Holmes, stating that if Holmes would only "hint to Brandeis that judicial opinions aren't to be written in the form of a brief it would be a great relief to the world."[51] Whether Holmes ever made such a suggestion to his colleagues is not known. If he did, it was taken very lightly, because Brandeis continued to write frequent opinions containing voluminous information from extra-legal authorities throughout the remainder of his tenure on the Supreme Court.[52]

Although the "Brandeis opinion" did not serve as a model for the opinions of other justices on the Court until the second half of Brandeis's term of service, it did provide an opening wedge for the judicial reliance upon extensive extra-legal information that began in the 1930s. When the so-called "legal realists" of the Depression years began to urge greater legal appreciation of social science information, they frequently alluded to the pioneering use of statistics and expert testimony in Brandeis's early opinions. Moreover, Brandeis's laborious (although often diffuse) research while on the bench may have provided inspiration for the forages into extra-legal sources of information by later justices such as Black, Douglas, and Frankfurter.[53]

Brandeis's service to the rise of an informational paradigm in American law can also be discussed in terms of his peculiar use of law clerks while a member of the Supreme Court. One of the most remarkable things about Brandeis's landmark dissent in the 1917 *Adams* case is that the recently appointed justice performed the substantial extra-legal research for his opinion entirely on his own. The briefs of counsel were of very little help.[54] This was not unusual: appellate attorneys appearing before the Supreme Court in the period between the two world wars seldom alluded to extra-legal authorities or information in their briefs.[55] So Brandeis sought assistance elsewhere for his research into such authorities. To enable him to write the types of information-laden opinions that he believed were needed, Brandeis turned to his law clerks. Shortly after his solo research effort in the *Adams* case, Brandeis began calling upon his law clerks to assist him in undertaking extra-legal as well as legal research.

Law clerks, essentially highly skilled research assistants, were first provided for Supreme Court justices by an 1886 Act of Congress.[56] Brandeis was the first justice to ask his law clerks to scour libraries for authorities and information outside of the traditional case reports, statute books, and legal treatises. Brandeis's usual practice was to have his law clerks perform much of the extra-legal research and then write the footnotes to his opinions.[57] After Brandeis revised his opinions—some as many as twenty times—he asked his clerks to check the revisions against the pleadings and the evidence. If additional research or documentation was called for to bolster the revised opinions, the clerks performed such tasks.[58] Justice Stone, who served on the Supreme Court from 1925 to 1946 (the last five years as Chief Justice), was the contemporary of Brandeis on the Court most willing to follow Brandeis's example of asking his law clerks to perform extra-legal research.[59]

Brandeis's clerks were selected by Felix Frankfurter from the roster of top recent graduates of the Harvard Law School; Brandeis accepted all of Frankfurter's suggested candidates sight unseen. Among Brandeis's law clerks were men who later became some of the most able legal scholars and public figures of the first half of the twentieth century: Dean Acheson (Secretary of State under Truman), James Landis (dean of the Harvard Law School), Circuit

Judge Calvert Magruder, and law professors Henry Hart, Jr., Paul Freund, Louis Jaffe, David Riesman, and J. Willard Hurst.[60] Most of these distinguished individuals came to share Brandeis's belief in the value of a "jurisprudence of facts" rather than one of concepts. In their writings and in their public service they came to appreciate the role of extra-legal information in the judicial process. Landis, for example, in the 1930s was a leading advocate of the use of extra-legal materials such as the debates of Congress in the judicial construction of statutes.[61] Riesman, a well-known sociologist as well as a law professor, became a partisan of the use of social science data in the legal process.[62] And Hurst, the country's dean of legal historians, has done as much as any one person in this century to examine how American law has been informed by social and economic conditions.[63]

The Intellectual Role of Extra-Legal Evidence for Louis Brandeis

Although Brandeis's use of extra-legal sources of information in his appellate briefs and post-1916 Supreme Court opinions certainly served strategic legal purposes, it is plausible that it also fulfilled an idiosyncratic intellectual need for Brandeis as a person. At the risk of engaging in a bit of psychobiography, it can be suggested that Brandeis's devotion to information-laden briefs and opinions allowed him to come to terms with two seemingly contradictory intellectual tenets peculiar to him as an individual. Brandeis was, at the same time, a moralist and a person who prized detachment. His experience as a consumer-oriented attorney and, in later years, as a committed Zionist points to his strong convictions about right and wrong. Yet, shortly after taking his seat on the High Court, Brandeis established himself as one of the great judicial self-restrainers in the Court's history. His concurring opinion in *Ashwander* v. *T.V.A.*[64]—in which the justice outlined "a series of rules" for the avoidance of constitutional questions—is one of the classic apologies in American legal history for judicial circumspection. How could two such apparently diverse sets of opinions reside in the mind of one person?

Brandeis found a way of reconciling these diverse beliefs by means of his commitment to facts and extra-legal information. His factually laden "Brandeis briefs" and "Brandeis opinions" allowed him occasional opportunities to vent his passions while still maintaining the impression of detachment. All of his appellate briefs that drew extensively upon extra-legal information were filed in support of state laws; almost all of his similarly information-oriented Supreme Court opinions were issued in dissent, but in support of state labor laws that the Court's majority voted to strike down. By providing statistical or "scientific" evidence as justification for such laws, Brandeis's briefs and opinions may have appeared to some of his contemporaries as objective documents. At times, Brandeis himself even seemed to think that his acquired information spoke for itself.[65] Yet, behind the statistics and the testimony always lurked Brandeis's strongly held convictions regarding right and wrong. He seldom permitted those convictions to be called into the service of overruling a law he thought to be unwise. But in defense of a statute he thought had merit, or in support of a law that a legislature had enacted after a careful study of social and economic conditions, Brandeis could and did express himself strongly. Given the proper circumstances, Brandeis's information-packed documents became the texts for the economic and social lessons that he wanted to drive home to the legal community. Louis Jaffe, one of the Justice's former law clerks who later became a law professor, put it this way:

Brandeis preferred the sermon to the sword, reasoned counsel to the exercise of power, however reasonable. He put his hopes in education, in experience. Though he was a man of action, he was equally a teacher; he did not greatly care to lead people by the nose.[66]

As a teacher, Brandeis's principal pedagogical canon was that all action, particularly legal action, should be founded upon a reasonable factual basis. It was Brandeis's devotion to the jurisprudence of facts that led him to initiate and sponsor wide-ranging searches for information bearing upon existing social and economic conditions. It was Brandeis, more than any other legal figure of the early twentieth century, who was responsible for the accession of the informational mind-set in American law.

Notes

1. The case in which Brandeis made this argument was *Stettler* v. *O'Hara*, 243 U.S. 629 (1916). Ironically, Brandeis was appointed to the Supreme

Court shortly after the oral argument in the case and was, therefore, unable to participate in the voting on the constitutionality of the law. Without his vote, the Court divided evenly, four to four, and the Act was upheld.

2. William Hitz to Felix Frankfurter, December 1944, quoted in Clement Vose, "The National Consumers' League and the Brandeis Brief," 1 *Midwest Journal of Political Science* 267, 280 (1962).

3. 208 U.S. 412 (1908).

4. An intriguing discussion of the role of so-called "great men" in accomplishing social change is found in Lawrence M. Friedman and Jack Ladinsky, "Social Change and the Law of Industrial Accidents," 67 *Columbia Law Review* 51, 78-79 (1967).

5. Louis Brandeis and Josephine Goldmark, *Women in Industry . . . Brief for the State of Oregon* (New York, 1908).

6. See generally Alpheus T. Mason, *Brandeis: Lawyer and Judge in the Modern State* (Princeton, 1933), pp. 102-122; Vose, "The National Consumers' League and the Brandeis Brief"; and Paul L. Rosen, *The Supreme Court and Social Science* (Urbana, Ill., 1972), pp. 75-87, et passim.

7. 198 U.S. 45 (1905).

8. Brandeis and Goldmark, pp. 9-10

9. Ibid., p. 9. See also *Lochner v. New York*, 198 U.S. 45, 53, 67 (1905).

10. Alpheus T. Mason, "The Case of the Overworked Laundress," in John Garraty, ed., *Quarrels that Have Shaped the Constitution* (New York, 1975), p. 179.

11. *Amicus curiae* translates literally "friend of the court." An *amicus curiae* is a brief submitted by a party not directly involved in the litigation but interested in the outcome of a case. Most *amici* briefs are drafted by large organizations or pressure groups. The privilege of filing *amici* briefs is governed by rules set down by the Supreme Court. See generally Samuel Krislov, "The *Amicus Curiae* Brief: From Friendship to Advocacy," 72 *Yale Law Journal* 694 (1963); Clement Vose, *Constitutional Change: Amendment Politics and Supreme Court Litigation Since 1900* (Lexington, Mass., 1972), passim. Cf. Nathan Hakman, "Lobbying the Supreme Court—An Appraisal of 'Political Science Folklore,' " 35 *Fordham Law Review* 15 (1966).

12. On Brandeis's career before his appointment to the Supreme Court, see esp. Alpheus T. Mason, *Brandeis: A Free Man's Life* (New York, 1946), pp. 99-464.

13. The best discussion of the role of Josephine Goldmark and the National Consumers' League in assembling the brief for the *Muller* appeal is Vose, "The National Consumers' League and the Brandeis Brief."

14. Brandeis and Goldmark, pp. 9-10,113

15. *Muller v. Oregon*, at 420.

16. Josephine Goldmark, *Impatient Crusader: Florence Kelly's Life Story* (Urbana, Ill., 1953), p. 155.

17. *Jay Burns Baking Co.* v. *Bryan*, 264 U.S. 504, 520 (1924) (Brandeis & Holmes, JJ., dissenting).

18. See Mason, *Brandeis: A Free Man's Life*, pp. 245-253; and Henry Wolf Biklé, "Judicial Determination of Questions of Fact Affecting the Constitutional Validity of Legislative Action," 38 *Harvard Law Review* 6 (1924).

19. Rosen, pp. 80-87.

20. National Consumers' League, *Thirty-Five Years of Crusading, 1899-1935* (New York, 1935), p. 10. A listing of the cases in which the League was involved can be found in Vose, "The National Consumers' League and the Brandeis Brief," 277, note 18. The discussion of the National Consumers' League's role in appellate court litigation that is contained in this chapter, except where indicated otherwise, relies upon the two authorities cited in this note.

21. 261 U.S. 525 (1923).

22. Vose, "The National Consumers' League and the Brandeis Brief," 281.

23. David Ziskind, "The Use of Economic Data in Labor Cases," 6 *University of Chicago Law Review* 607, 649-650 (1939).

24. 244 Ill. 509 (1910).

25. Josephine Goldmark, *Fatigue and Efficiency* (New York, 1912).

26. 243 U.S. 426 (1917).

27. (New York, 1925).

28. 300 U.S. 379 (1937).

29. See generally Leonard Baker, *Back to Back: The Duel Between FDR and the Supreme Court* (New York, 1967).

30. *Lochner* v. *New York*, 198 U.S. 45, 75 (1905) (Holmes, J., dissenting).

31. Although the original style Brandeis brief, documented heavily with statistics and economic testimony in support of state or Congressional labor laws, has rarely figured into Supreme Court litigation since 1937, a new type of Brandeis brief has appeared in the last generation. Since the late 1940s, attorneys in civil rights cases have frequently relied upon briefs studded with the extra-legal testimony of psychologists and sociologists. Unlike the original briefs, however, these new style Brandeis briefs have not been employed in support of remedial statutes. Rather, they have cited social scientific authority for the purpose of contesting racially discriminatory laws and social practices. On the "new" Brandeis briefs, see esp. Clement Vose, *Caucasians Only: The Supreme Court, the NAACP and the Restrictive Covenant Cases* (Berkeley, 1959), passim; Rosen, pp. 134-196; and Richard Kluger, *Simple Justice: The History of Brown v. Board of*

Education and Black America's Struggle for Equality (New York, 1975), pp. 315-345, et passim. See also Paul A. Freund, *The Supreme Court of the United States: Its Business, Purposes and Performance* (Cleveland, 1961), pp. 150-154, for a vigorous critique of the civil rights Brandeis briefs of the post-World War II period. Freund, an eminent constitutional scholar and a former law clerk for Justice Brandeis, believed that the new wave of Brandeis briefs, which cites pages of extra-legal authorities to challenge established laws and customs, perverts the purpose for which Brandeis himself intended such briefs. He noted that the extra-legal briefs of Brandeis and his pre-World War II disciples were employed in support of the constitutionality of regulatory legislation. Thus, according to Freund, briefs that employ extra-legal information and authorities to attack the constitutionality of legislation are not true Brandeis briefs. Freund's view is subjected to an excellent critique in Rosen, pp. 177-182.

32. *Muller* v. *Oregon*, at 420.

33. Ibid., at 419-420.

34. 244 U.S. 590 (1917). On the importance of Brandeis's dissent in *Adams*, see generally Chester A. Newland, "Innovation in Judicial Technique: The Brandeis Opinion," 42 *Southwestern Social Science Quarterly* 22 (1961).

35. 244 U.S. 590, 597 (Brandeis, J., dissenting).

36. Ibid., at 600 (Brandeis, J., dissenting).

37. Besides Brandeis's dissent in *Adams* v. *Tanner*, see esp. his similarly information-packed opinions in *New York Central R.R.* v. *Winfield*, 244 U.S. 147, 154 (1917) (Brandeis, J., dissenting); *Truax* v. *Corrigan*, 257 U.S. 312, 354 (1921) (Brandeis, J., dissenting); *Southwestern Bell Tel. Co.* v. *Public Service Comm.*, 262 U.S. 276, 289 (1923) (Brandeis, J., dissenting); *St. Louis and O'Fallon Ry.* v. *United States*, 279 U.S. 461, 488 (1929) (Brandeis, J., dissenting); *United Railways and Electric Co.* v. *West*, 280 U.S. 234, 255 (1930) (Brandeis, J., dissenting); *New State Ice Co.* v. *Liebmann*, 285 U.S. 262, 280 (1932) (Brandeis, J., dissenting); and *Liggett* v. *Lee*, 288 U.S. 517, 541 (1933) (Brandeis, J., dissenting).

38. 257 U.S. 312 (1921).

39. Ibid., 257 U.S. 312, 354, at 356-357 (1921) (Brandeis, J., dissenting).

40. Mason, *Brandeis: Lawyer and Judge in the Modern State*, p. 129.

41. These reactions to Wilson's nomination of Brandeis to the Supreme Court are merely samples of the rich range of comment sparked by the President's surprising announcement. Mason, *Brandeis: A Free Man's Life*, pp. 465-470.

42. See Jerold S. Auerbach, *Unequal Justice: Lawyers and Social Change in Modern America* (New York, 1976), pp. 102-129.

43. Mason, *Brandeis: A Free Man's Life*, pp. 470-508.

44. Ibid., p. 518.

45. This terminology was first suggested by Brandeis himself in a 1916 address to the Chicago Bar Association, titled "The Living Law." The text of the speech was later published under the same title in 10 *Illinois Law Review* 461 (1916). Brandeis's leading biographer, Alpheus T. Mason, made good use of these polar terms in discussing how Brandeis differed from most of his contemporaries. See *Brandeis: Lawyer and Judge in the Modern State*, passim.

46. Note, "Employment Agencies Forbidden to Take Fees from Workers," 27 *Yale Law Journal* 134, 135 (1917).

47. Quoted in Mason, *Brandeis: A Free Man's Life*, p. 518.

48. The case was *U.S.* v. *Robbins*, 269 U.S. 315 (1926). The justice citing law review authority in this case was Oliver Wendell Holmes. This is slightly surprising because Holmes seldom cited as authorities any extra-legal sources in his written Supreme Court opinions.

49. John W. Johnson, "The Dimensions of Non-Legal Evidence in the American Judicial Process: The United States Supreme Court's Use of Extra-Legal Materials in the Twentieth Century" (Unpublished Ph.D. Dissertation: University of Minnesota, 1974), pp. 194-207.

50. Mason, *Brandeis: A Free Man's Life*, pp. 517-518.

51. Mark DeWolfe Howe, ed., *Holmes-Laski Letters* (Cambridge, Mass., 1953), I, p. 127.

52. See esp. Brandeis's opinions in the cases cited *supra*, note 37. See also Mason, *Brandeis: Lawyer and Judge in the Modern State*, pp. 124-173, 180-185.

53. See, for example, William O. Douglas, *Go East, Young Man: The Early Years* (New York, 1974), pp. 441-449, for Douglas's own statements regarding Brandeis's general influence upon his own judicial practices and ideas.

54. Newland, "Innovation in Judicial Technique: The Brandeis Opinion," 24.

55. Johnson, "The Dimensions of Non-Legal Evidence in the American Judicial Process," 215-220.

56. 24 Stat. 254 (1886). On the use of law clerks by Supreme Court justices, see generally Chester A. Newland, "Personal Assistants to Supreme Court Justices: The Law Clerks," 40 *Oregon Law Review* 299 (1961).

57. Ibid., 314-315. See also Dean Acheson, "Reflections of Service with the Federal Supreme Court," 18 *Alabama Lawyer* 355 (1957).

58. Alpheus T. Mason, "Louis D. Brandeis," in Leon Friedman and Fred L. Israel, eds. *The Justices of the United States Supreme Court, 1789-1969: Their Lives and Major Opinions* (New York, 1969), III, p. 2058.

59. See Alpheus T. Mason, *Harlan Fiske Stone: Pillar of the Law* (New York, 1956), p. 513.

60. Mason, *Brandeis: A Free Man's Life*, p. 690.

61. See esp. his article, "A Note on 'Statutory Interpretation,' " 43 *Harvard Law Review* 886 (1930).

62. This is most clearly revealed in his review essay on a social science-oriented law school textbook, "Law and Social Science: A Report on Michael and Wechsler's Classbook on Criminal Law and Administration," 50 *Yale Law Journal* 636 (1940).

63. The first two issues of volume 10 of the *Law and Society Review* contain seven essays published in honor of Hurst. At the end of the second issue is a bibliography that contains an enumeration of Hurst's publications through 1974 and a list of the reviews of his major works: see Ronald Eskin and Robert Hayden, "James Willard Hurst: A Bibliography," 10 *Law and Society Review* 325 (1976).

64. 297 U.S. 288, 346 (1936) (Brandeis, J., concurring).

65. See my discussion of this point, *supra*, this chapter.

66. Louis Jaffe, "Was Brandeis an Activist? The Search for Intermediate Premises," 80 *Harvard Law Review* 986, 989 (1967).

4
NEW SOURCES OF INFORMATION: SUPPLANTING THE COMMON LAW

With any case before an appellate court, three broad avenues of legal interpretation are possible. The court is asked either to apply precedents in common law or equity, to construe the meaning of a statute as it affects the case at bar, or to find guidance in a constitutional provision to help decide the case. These three categories of construction may be termed, for the purposes of this examination, *common law construction*, *statutory construction*, and *constitutional construction*. Many cases decided by written opinion in appellate courts involve, at various points in the judges' rationales, two or even all three of these modes of construction. Usually, though, one form predominates.

Justice Felix Frankfurter—one of the legal figures of the twentieth century most sensitive to the role of extra-legal information in the American judicial process—once estimated that strictly common law-oriented cases comprised over 40 percent of the U.S. Supreme Court's business as late as 1875. But, he claimed, by the end of World War II, cases arising out of the unvarnished common law had virtually disappeared from the High Court's docket.[1] A statistical survey of Supreme Court opinions written between 1925 and 1969 bears out Frankfurter's suspicions regarding the decline of common law litigation in the Supreme Court's docket.[2] In the late 1920s, common law construction was found to be the principal form of legal interpretation in an average of 19.8 percent of the cases decided by full opinion per Term; in the 1960s, the frequency of cases decided by full opinion that had a primary common law bent averaged only 7.4 percent per Term. The decline in the relative status of common law litigation in the Supreme Court from the 1920s to the late 1960s was a product of the changing nature of the Court's business. Statutory-oriented litigation, which by the late 1920s already accounted for two-thirds of the Court's full-dress cases, remained at a high level as late as the 1960s. But it was the dramatic growth of litigation involving primarily constitutional issues that supplanted common law-oriented appellate cases. In the late 1920s, only an average of 14.2 percent of the cases per Term demanded constitutional interpretation as the primary mode of legal construction. By the October Terms of the 1960s, fully one-third of all of the Court's cases decided by full opinions involved essentially constitutional issues.[3] The decline of common law litigation and the rise of constitutionally oriented cases between 1925 and 1970 have been far from regular. Nevertheless, a marked change has occurred in the frequency of the types of legal construction in cases decided by the High Court.

Associated with the decline of common law-oriented Supreme Court cases and the rise of constitutional adjudication is another phenomenon. Between 1925 and 1970, the number of appellate court opinions relying upon what may be termed "extra-legal information" increased substantially. This term, as used here, refers to those categories of authorities that do not have the force of law. Such extra-legal authorities were and are cited in appellate court opinions for their informational and persuasive value. They are referred to and expanded upon by judges and lawyers because they can provide useful information or suggest desirable lines of legal action. They are meant to be only suggestive of what "the law" is or should be. In short, they may be, in a loose sense, "legal authorities," but they are not "legally authoritative."

Those extra-legal authorities that convey information or suggest policy alternatives include legal treatises and other published books, articles from legal periodicals and nonlegal journals, legal encyclopedias and other compilations of legal principles, legislative committe reports or the records of legislative debates, and unpublished documents such as letters or manuscripts. This catalog is by no means exhaustive. Some judges, as noted previously, have been known to cite "authorities" from classical antiquity in support of various points.[4] But the categories just mentioned have been the leading groups of extra-legal authorities consulted by American appellate courts.

Many of the types of extra-legal authority that are important to appellate courts today were frabricated by the legal community itself between 1910 and 1940. In fact, in no other period of American legal history were so many "new sources" of extra-legal information created. The significance of these sources was first grasped—and then only partially—by law professor Max Radin in 1928. Writing in the maiden volume of the *Southern California Law Review*, Professor Radin, one of the most vigorous critics of the conventional wisdoms of American law in the interwar years, began his article with the observation that modern American appellate courts had recently begun to rely upon an exceptionally large number of technically "nonlegal" authorities as sources of the law:

There are scarcely 10 pages of the Reporter [volume 158 of the *Northeastern Reporter*] in which some treatises do not appear and certainly not 10 in which there is no reference to one of the many existing cyclopedias, repertories, handbooks, or digests or dictionaries.[5]

Radin was critical of the courts for depending too heavily upon "authorities" that were only meant to be labor-saving tools, designed to assist attorneys and judges in their research and not intended to be cited as literal sources of the law. On the other hand, he was favorably impressed by the small but rapidly increasing judicial cognizance of scholarly articles in the university law journals.

Ignoring for the moment Radin's qualitative assessment of the "new sources of the law," the concern now need be only with Radin's nonjudgmental statement that courts in the late 1920s were looking to several novel places for legal authority—including encyclopedias, repertoires, treatises (new and old), articles in legal periodicals, legal handbooks, case digests, and law dictionaries—

and directly acknowledging these sources in the bodies of appellate court opinions. Of the "new sources" noted by Radin, all, with the exception of treatises and law review articles, offered statements of then current legal principles and precedents, founded upon the bedrock of case law. Their compilers devised these sources to help the legal profession locate appropriate case precedents. They were fashioned from the common law, reflected the case precedents, and attempted to bring order to the myriad of reported cases. Their sundry compilers did not, in all likelihood, expect them to be used by attorneys and courts of law as legal authorities, much less as substitutes for the case precedents upon which they were supposedly based. Nevertheless, as Radin pointed out, they were so used.[6] An examination of the origin and nature of some of these "new sources" should help to illustrate this important dimension of the informational penchant of the early twentieth-century American legal community.

Legal Encyclopedias, Encyclopedic Treatises, and Annotated Reports

Although legal encyclopedias have long been published in this country and in England, the period between the two world wars is noteworthy because it marked the development and initial publication of the most sophisticated and comprehensive legal encyclopedias in American history. Appearing first in this period was the legal encyclopedia *Corpus Juris*, originally published by the American Law Book Company of Brooklyn, New York. Its first edition was issued in 1913. Its objective, as stated in the preface to its revised edition, was "to make available a more efficient and more complete presentation of the entire body of the law as it now exists in the many thousands of volumes of reported cases."[7] Furthermore, the compilers of the revised edition of *Corpus Juris*, published as *Corpus Juris Secundum* in 1936 by West Publishing Company of St. Paul, Minnesota, repeated the maxim of the first edition: "If it is in the reported cases, it is in *Corpus Juris*; if it is not in *Corpus Juris*, it is not in the reported cases."[8] In short, *Corpus Juris* claimed to "cover all the cases and cite all the cases" in the American past, dating to the first reported case in 1658.

Similar to a general encyclopedia, the volumes of *Corpus Juris* and *Corpus Juris Secundum* are organized alphabetically by subject heading. Each subject heading is divided and subdivided almost ad infinitum. To each subdivision are appended footnotes of relevant cases that, supposedly, provide the authority for the legal points raised in the section. The discussions of the law for each subject are authored by anonymous individuals. The fact that most of the authors chosen for the first edition of *Corpus Juris* were laymen or run-of-the-mill lawyers makes the discussions of the law somewhat suspect.[9] However, references to substantive discussions in *Corpus Juris* frequently found their way into briefs and judicial opinions as early as the 1920s.[10] *Corpus Juris* served as the approximate model for the other synoptic and generally more astute legal encyclopedia, *American Jurisprudence*, first published in 1936 by the Lawyers' Cooperative Publishing Company of Rochester, New York. The success of *American Jurisprudence* and *Corpus Juris* encouraged several states to bring out legal encyclopedias applicable to their particular legal environments.

The early twentieth century also witnessed the appearance of multivolume legal treatises such as John Wigmore on *Evidence*[11] and Samuel Williston on *Contracts*,[12] which were, for all intents and purposes, encyclopedic treatments of specialized subjects. Williston's monumental treatise on contracts appeared first in a four-volume edition in 1919. In the early thirties, Williston and a series of assistants began work on a revised edition that ultimately grew to eight volumes, the last appearing in 1938. The revised edition of Williston on *Contracts* contained an alphabetical table of over seventy thousand cases that comprised, by itself, an entire volume. In Williston's autobiography, *Life and Law*, he included a "poetic review" of his treatise that had originally appeared in *The New York Tribune:*

> When Freudian novels clog the brain,
>   And modern verse is found too antic,
> This little book will entertain
>   The Realist and the Romantic.
> The author often deals with sex,
> Yet in a way that does not vex.

> The characters are mainly three,
> But in a thousand lights you view them.
> There are but A and B and C,
> Though sometimes D is added to them.
> Such vigor animates the four,
> I do not think you'll wish for more.
>
> Each plays a multitude of parts,
> And sheds his aspect like a fairy.
> An offeree he gayly starts,
> And ends a beneficiary!
> To find out how the thing is done
> Will furnish you with loads of fun.
>
> Besides the tale the author tells,
> He swells your stock of information,
> His brief remarks on Dean Langdell's
> Discussion of consideration
> Should be persued—I put it mild-
> Ly—by each woman, man and child.
>
> The tome's extremely worth your while.
> It's clearly printed, light, and well bound.
> The lucid and emphatic style
> Will capture you and hold you spellbound.
> I don't exaggerate its powers—
> It holds me every night for hours.[13]

The critic may have been too enamored of Williston's "lucid and emphatic style," but he justly praises the "stock of information" provided in the treatise.

Since legal encyclopedias tend to be general, discursive, and occasionally inaccurate, they are not as readily referred to by lawyers and judges as another source of extra-legal information, the annotated report. Annotated reports attempt to compile the relatively small number of cases that have special significance in deciding substantive questions and contribute to the development and growth of a nation's law. In the United States, the most comprehensive and scholarly annotated reports series, the *American Law Reports* (ALR), compiled by the Lawyers' Cooperative Publishing Company, went into publication in 1919. Its immense success with the legal profession is partially indicated by the fact that it is now in its third series and is the only set of annotated reports currently being edited. ALR contains certain features that render it superior to general encyclopedias. First, it reprints a leading appellate court opinion for each of hundreds of subdivisions within its scores of volumes. For each "leading case," summaries and "headnotes" (major points of law) are included, as are summaries of briefs of counsel. It is more exhaustive and better referenced to court decisions, by separate jurisdictions, than the normal encyclopedic discussions. Second, it is compiled by an expert—either someone experienced in the editing of law reports or an experienced lawyer. The ALR annotations are analytic as well as synthetic. Thoughtful value judgments and legal prescriptions are not forsworn. Often the opinions of an annotator in the ALR have presaged important legal innovations. Judges look kindly upon "ALR cites," and they consider themselves fortunate indeed if one of their opinions is chosen for inclusion in the ALR as a "leading case." Even in the 1920s, ALR discussions were already being cited in appellate court opinions.[14]

It should be reiterated that legal encyclopedias, lengthy treatises, and annotated reports were not intended by their editors and compilers to serve as primary sources of the law. That is, they were not expected to be set forth in briefs and court opinions as the equivalent of case authority. The fact that the discussions in these volumes were occasionally relied upon by appellate courts in lieu of case authority must have surprised even the proudest formulators of these "legal research tools." Yet, another type of legal compilation appeared in the interwar years that had as its avowed purpose the substitution of its own authority for that of the common law. This "new source of the law" warrants separate consideration.

The Restatement of the Law

Clearly, the most ambitious "new source" of the law created in the period 1910-40 was the "Restatement," a codelike compilation of legal principles assembled by some of the country's most distinguished law professors. The Restatement volumes were products of a mammoth undertaking, costing millions of dollars and requiring the work of scores of the best conceptual legal minds in America. The Restatement effort still continues today.

The movement for a "restatement of the common law" grew out of a fairly widespread frustration around the turn of the century among appellate judges and law professors with the complexity and lack of uniformity of American case law. Samuel Williston, one of the leading "Restaters," estimated that the number of volumes of American appellate court cases had increased from about thirty-five hundred in 1885 to almost nine thousand by the beginning of World War I,[15] thus making the sheer bulk of the case law almost overwhelming. Furthermore, statistics gathered by the American Bar Association in the 1880s indicated that about one-half of the country's appellate court decisions resulted in the reversals of trial court decisions,[16] suggesting that the courts of first instance or the appellate courts—or both—were misinformed about or unfamiliar with the applicable law in far too many circumstances.

In 1914, at a meeting of the Association of American Law Schools (AALS), two papers were delivered by prestigious authors that offered some pregnant suggestions on how to come to terms with the bulk and conflicting nature of American case law. One paper, titled "The Vital School of Jurisprudence and Law," was read by Wesley Hohfeld of the Yale Law School; the other, titled "The Necessity for a Study of the Legal System," was proffered by Joseph H. Beale of Harvard. In the following year, Dean H.S. Richards of the University of Wisconsin Law School, in his presidential address to the AALS, expressed the hope that the papers by Hohfeld and Beale might spark the establishment of a center for the "systematization and study"—by judges, practitioners, and teachers—of the "broad lines of American and English jurisprudence." The dreams of Hohfeld, Beale, and Richards eventually were realized with the founding of the American Law Institute (ALI) in 1923.[17]

The ALI sought to fashion tools by which lawyers and judges would be able to ascertain quickly the most authoritative precedents in given areas of the law, thus obliterating eccentricities from the common law and promoting doctrinal unity throughout the country. The Institute set about its work by appointing "reporters" and "committees of advisors" in various subject areas of the law to compile volumes containing the "correct" legal principles. The first offering to appear was the multivolume *Restatement of the Law of Contracts*, published in 1932.[18] By 1945 Restatements had been published for eight other subject areas of case law: agency, conflict of laws, judgments, property, restitution, security, torts, and trusts. Since World War II, the ALI has been occupied in issuing other Restatements and restatements of Restatements, that is, "Second Restatements."

The Restatements do not make particularly fascinating reading. They are weighty volumes containing statements of what most courts, which have ruled upon a particular question, have held to be "the law." The statements are expressed in black-letter, statutory form. Explanation, illustration, commentary, and case citations—although included—are definitely secondary to the *ex cathedra* "majority principles." The "Restaters," unlike the editors of the other "new sources" of the law in the early twentieth century, believed their repertoires would be able to command an authority greater than any treatise or specialized encylcopedia, "an authority more nearly on a par with that accorded the decisions of courts."[19] Williston, the reporter for the *Restatement of Contracts*, believed the Restatements would crowd out common law authority, show courts that were out of line with the authority of the Restatement the error of their ways, and some day provide an excellent foundation for a legal code.[20]

In spite of the tremendous expenditures of time, money, and intelligence, the authority of the Restatement did not come to hold as much sway as the original formulators believed likely. The Restatements did not supplant common law authority, but even as vehement a critic of the Restaters as Thurman Arnold of the Yale Law School acknowledged that the Restatement had become by the mid-1930s "an additional source of argument."[21] The various court decisions that cited Restatement provisions—not the Restatement's black-letter statements themselves—remained the authoritative sources of the law. Nevertheless, as statistics compiled by the American Law Institute demonstrate, the Restatement quickly became an important source of guidance and information for lawyers and appellate judges. Between 1932 and 1950, provisions of the Restatement were cited almost eighteen thousand times by federal and state appellate courts.[22] Much to their surprise, the Restaters found from their own follow-up research that much less conflict existed among the laws of the several states than most of the legal community had previously thought to be the case. Between 1932 and 1945, fewer than 2 percent of the state court holdings surveyed by the ALI were found to be contrary to the Restatement text.[23] So instead of becoming a legal Occam's razor, cutting away the eccentricities of the common law and simplifying legal doctrine, the Restatement eventually came to function as just another research tool, reporting merely what the common law was in fact in most jurisdictions. Yet, the informative value of the Restatement should not be underestimated. The approximate one thousand appellate court references a year in the 1930s and 1940s is testimony enough to the worth of the Restatements to the American legal community.

The efforts of the restaters might have been more helpful to the legal community if it had not been for the Depression of the 1930s. Explanatory treatises were proposed by the ALI to complement and reinforce the authority of the Restatement's most important sections. But the national economic plight caused foundation funds, upon which the Restatement project sorely depended, to diminish markedly. Rather than limit the breadth of coverage of the Restatement, the Institute simply abandoned its plans for the projected treatises.[24] Commentary in such treatises might have served the useful purpose of informing the legal community that the black-letter rules of the Restatement grew out of specific social and economic milieus. However, given the conceptual bent of the leading Restaters—most of whom were professors in the Harvard Law School and still enamored with the formalistic jurisprudence of Langdell[25]—it is doubtful that even if such treatises had been forthcoming that they would have emphasized the manifold relationships of law and its social context.

The Law Reviews

In 1887 a group of Harvard Law Students decided that some of the legal essays they had been sharing with each other in a "little

club'' were worthy of publication. Thus was the inauspicious beginning of the *Harvard Law Review*, the first student-edited legal
journal in America. The group of students there at the creation of
this seminal publication included John Wigmore, later dean of the
Northwestern University Law School and author of the monumental treatise on evidence; Julian Mack, later a United States
circuit judge; and Joseph Beale and Samuel Williston, later to be
distinguished Harvard law professors.[26] Early issues of the *Review*
contained articles by leading legal scholars as well as student--
authored case notes and comments. Several articles in the first few
volumes should be best forgotten.[27] However, a few articles, such
as "The Right to Privacy," written by Samuel Warren and Louis
Brandeis in the fourth volume,[28] are still regarded as classics. Also
included in the early issues were abstracts of notes taken by law
students from the lectures of their professors.[29] Mercifully, after a
few years, the practice of replicating lecture notes disappeared
from the *Review*. But the other features of the *Review* were retained
and still exist today. Harvard's publication became the model for
scholarly publications in other law schools. Soon, every law school—
particularly every new law school looking to establish its credi-
bility—moved to found a law review.

The first issue of the *Harvard Law Review* contained a brief
editorial note, stating in part that ". . . we are not without hopes
that the *Review* may be serviceable to the profession at large."[30]
Despite these high expectations, it was some time before the American legal community paid serious attention to the law reviews.
About 1910 Justice Holmes, who was a member of the Harvard
Law School faculty a few years before the founding of the *Review*,
admonished an attorney appearing before the Supreme Court to
avoid citing as authority "the work of boys."[31] It was not until
1917 that a member of the U.S. Supreme Court made mention of a
law review article in a written opinion. The justice was, not surprisingly, Louis Brandeis; the case was the previously discussed
employment agency case, *Adams* v. *Tanner*.[32] Brandeis quickly
became the leading advocate of the use of law review authority on
the appellate bench. By the time he had retired from the Supreme
Court, Brandeis had authored forty-seven opinions in which law
review articles were cited.[33] Between 1917 and the end of the 1929

Term of the Court, law review articles had been cited by various justices in twenty-nine cases; they were cited in seventy-one cases during the 1930s.[34]

Although law review authority did not inform the views of appellate judges in the first third of the twentieth century to the degree that the other "new sources" of the law did, the reviews did provide crucial information and suggest instructive lines of legal analysis in a few important cases. For example, in *Whitney* v. *California*,[35] a case dealing with a state law that made it a crime to be part of a group advocating "criminal syndicalism," Justice Brandeis's concurring opinion cited with favor a law review article by Charles Warren.[36] Although Brandeis was led to agree with the decision of the Court that the California law was constitutional, he was willing to go further than the other members of the Court in applying the Fourteenth Amendment's Due Process Clause as a tool to evaluate state laws restricting the freedom of speech.[37] Here, he drew support from Warren's historical analysis of the Bill of Rights and the Fourteenth Amendment.[38] In another landmark free-speech decision of the period, *Near* v. *Minnesota*,[39] the majority opinion, authored by Chief Justice Hughes, made mention of a law review article by Roscoe Pound.[40]

Without question, the most extensive and consequential use of law review authority by the U.S. Supreme Court in the first decades of the twentieth century was in a 1938 decision authored by Justice Brandeis, *Erie* v. *Tompkins*.[41] the case involved the alleged negligence of the Erie Railroad in causing an accident to a man named Tompkins who, while walking near a railroad line, was struck by a passing train of the Erie Railroad. The question raised was whether the suit of Tompkins's in the federal courts would be governed by the Pennsylvania common law of negligence or the "federal common law" that had developed since the 1842 Supreme Court decision of *Swift* v. *Tyson*.[42] In overruling the nineteenth-century precedent and holding that no such entity as federal common law existed, Brandeis referred to scores of law review articles that were critical of the rule in *Swift* v. *Tyson*.[43] In particular, he relied upon Charles Warren's lengthy article, "New Light on the History of the Federal Judiciary Act of 1789."[44] According to Warren, the drafters of the Judiciary Act[45] did not intend to open the door for an exten-

sive body of federal common law. Rather, they intended that a
federal court exercising jurisdiction in diversity of citizenship cases
(cases involving parties from two different states) would apply the
common law of the state in which it is situated except when a con-
trolling federal law applies. Besides being replete with information
about the views of the founding fathers, Warren's article contained
perceptive analyses of the differences between language in the
Judiciary Act and a recently discovered "Draft Bill." In essence,
by looking closely at the statutory language, Warren demonstrated
conclusively that the drafters of the crucial Section 34 had not
meant to establish a separate domain of federal common law.[46]
Relying upon Warren's information and argumentation, Brandeis
wrote the thesis of this law review article into the law, thus altering
substantially from that time forward the nature of litigation in the
federal courts.[47]

The use of law review information and analysis in appellate court
opinions drew a good bit of comment from members of the legal
community. Max Radin, in his 1928 article on the "new sources"
of the law, expressed general satisfaction with the recent disposal
of some lawyers and appellate court judges to cite law review authority. In fact, he even urged judges to be more willing to benefit
from the writings of men of "authoritative calibre" included in the
law reviews.[48] To Radin, the leading articles in major law reviews
were authoritatively superior to legal encyclopedias and annotated
reports.[49] Justice Cardozo, in 1931, wrote that law reviews were
becoming more and more respected as authorities in their own right
because, as he put it, leadership in legal thought was passing "from
the benches of the courts to the chairs of the universities."[50] He
noted that this supposed change in jurisprudential leadership had
stimulated a willingness of lawyers and judges increasingly to seek
information and guidance from law review essays.[51] Chief Justice
Taft, however, spoke for the conservative legal establishment in the
1920s when he chided some of his colleagues —principally Brandeis,
Stone, and Holmes—for the "undignified use" of law review
material in their dissents.[52] Although a substantial body of law
review writings existed in the twenties that would have suited conservative judges like Taft,[53] no evidence can be found that Taft
and his like-minded brethen relied upon such authority.[54] So the

information provided by law reviews in the 1920s and 1930s was clearly of more use to the judicial "liberals," such as Brandeis and Stone of the Federal Supreme Court.

New Sources of Information and the New Legal Community

The first four decades of the twentieth century witnessed the germination and blossoming of a bright array of "new sources" of the law. In no other period of American legal history were so many new sources of legal information fabricated. The two most comprehensive legal encyclopedias and some of the most influential multivolume sets of treatises were fashioned in the first third of the twentieth century. The most scholarly set of annotated reports—the only set still being kept up to date—and the monumental Restatement of American law had their origins in these years. Furthermore, the law reviews, which had their genesis in the late nineteenth century at a few Ivy League law schools, grew substantially in number and in quality in the interwar years, eventually serving to inform lawyers and appellate judges on a variety of subjects.

The obvious historical question to ask at this point is: Why did these new sources appear when they did? Or, why was the period between the world wars so conducive to the construction of these new sources of information and guidance? One answer was suggested at the outset of this chapter: the new types of cases coming before appellate courts in the early part of the twentieth century had something to do with the movement toward new types of authorities. Strictly common law-oriented litigation was declining, and statutory and constitutionally based litigation were becoming much more pronounced in the dockets of appellate courts. This shift might help explain the increasing influence of law reviews or legislative history on the courts. But the fact remains that most of the other "new sources" of the law created in the early twentieth century were designed to help find or to help interpret the common law. So the answer to the question of why these new sources developed when they did cannot be determined merely by examining the changing composition of appellate court dockets. A more comprehensive explanation can be obtained by considering also some of the changes that were occurring in the organization of the legal profession during these years.

It was in the first third of the twentieth century that the American legal community was undergoing what is usually termed "professionalization." During these years, elite American attorneys, judges, and law professors sought to bring a sense of order to the profession. In the early part of the century, the newly founded American Bar Association (ABA) and the Association of American Law Schools (AALS) were actively involved in upgrading the standards of admission to the law schools, standardizing the law school curriculum, setting higher barriers to be surmounted before admissions to state bars were granted, and promulgating rules of ethical behavior for attorneys.[55] Although it is fairly clear that some of the motivation for this professionalization was not of the highest order,[56] its principal consequence was to establish the law school as the "central institutional pathway into the legal profession."[57]

With law school attendance now rapidly becoming the main road to admission to the higher "castes" in the American bar, it became possible for the leading law schools to hire faculty on a permanent basis to teach and write about the law. Harvard began the trend of hiring full-time faculty in 1872 with the offer of a five-year contract to the twenty-six year old James Barr Ames, a young man who had had a brilliant law school record at Harvard but possessed little practical experiences at the bar. Following Harvard's lead, other major law schools moved away from the old model of instruction by lectures delivered by part-time practitioners and retired judges, complemented by student recitations of black-letter principles from textbooks. By World War I, the leading American law schools were staffed by full-time teachers of law, many of whom were quite young; almost all of this new generation employed the Langdell-inspired case method of instruction.[58] Thus, in the early twentieth century, for the first time in American history, a professional group of full-time law teachers existed whose commitment was to law in the abstract and who had the time and financial support to demonstrate their commitment in published form. From the pens of these men—the Willistons, the Wigmores, and the Beales—came many of the multivolume treatises of the early twentieth century and the greatest part of the Restatements of the law.

One of the concerns of the new law school professoriate can be seen as intellectually consistent with the activities of the practitioners and law school administrators. The concerted effort of the

ABA and the AALS in the early twentieth century to control the training, composition, and ethics of the legal profession provide the context for understanding the creation of so many new sources of information in the early twentieth century. That is, just as the ABA and the AALS wanted to move toward greater professional coherence and respectability in the period, certain factions within the profession wanted to bring greater order to legal doctrine. Both professionally and intellectually, then, the legal community in the early twentieth century was engaged in a "search for order."[59]

The case method of legal instruction contributed to the search for order. When Langdell and his Harvard faculty first began using the case method, they assumed it could serve as a device to bring a degree of coherence to the study of the law. In the preface to his first casebook, Langdell emphasized this very point:

It seemed to me . . . to be possible to take such a branch of the law as Contracts, for example, and . . . to select, classify, and arrange all the cases which had contributed in any important degree to the growth, development or establishment of any of its essential doctrines.[60]

As the law in the early twentieth century became more complicated and the number of appellate case reports grew virtually at a geometric rate, the case method as a rationalizing and classifying tool became more cherished. With the appointment in 1916 of Thomas Swan, a case method-trained Harvard law graduate, as the dean of the Yale Law School, all of the major American law schools had been converted to the case method.[61]

However, the case method proved to be a sword that cut two ways. On the one hand, as was discussed in chapter 2, the case method—at least in its early stages of adoption—served to confine law students and law professors to the study of appellate cases. Yet, by the second and third decades of the twentieth century, a number of the case method-trained law professors were busy authoring treatises, assisting in the compilation of encyclopedias, and serving as reporters or advisors for the Restatement project. Their goal in these endeavors was to fashion tools that would assist members of the legal community in finding the appropriate appellate court cases. However, as Radin pointed out in 1928, the new sources of legal information created by these men were frequently being substituted for common law authority in appellate briefs and judicial opinions. Thus, those responsible for these new sources may have performed their work too well. While being devoted to appellate court cases, they created sources that would help to diminish the authoritative bite of the common law.

Just as the case method sought to bring order to the law, so did the new sources of information created in this period. The Restaters, in particular, were caught up in a search for order in the formulation of their ambitious project. No one was more committed to the order promised by the Restatement than William D. Lewis, a professor at the University of Pennsylvania Law School in the early twentieth century and the person who, along with Samuel Williston, was appointed to prepare the first report on the desirability of undertaking a Restatement. In the course of a self-congratulatory article on the birth of the Restatement movement, titled "The History of the American Law Institute and the First Restatement of the Law: How We Did It," Lewis submitted that the principal impetus for the establishment of the American Law Institute and the Restatement was due to "a desire of the legal profession for an orderly statement of the common law."[62]

In retrospect, the search for order of the American legal profession in the early years of the twentieth century offers a good example of historical irony. A case method-trained professoriate, devoted to the scrutiny of appellate court cases as *the* route to an understanding of the law, devised several new sources of legal information intended to better this understanding and, hence, bring coherence to the study and practice of law. However, lawyers and appellate judges were so taken with the quality of these new sources of information that, instead of using them as research tools as they were generally intended by their formulators, they often referred to them in briefs and opinions as authorities in their own right, sometimes even in lieu of case authority. Furtermore, many of the new sources, far from convincing all members of the legal community that they provided satisfactory means of ordering the law, became grist for the cynical mills of the legal realists of the late twenties and the Depression. The retreat from order and the seeming embrace of chaos by the so-called legal realists—still, however, subservient to the efficacy of information in the legal process—is a subject explored at length in chapter 7.

Notes

1. Felix Frankfurter, "Reflections on Reading Statutes," in Alan Westin, ed., *An Autobiography of the Supreme Court: Off the Bench Commentary by the Justices* (New York, 1963), p. 306.

2. John W. Johnson, "The Dimensions of Non-Legal Evidence in the American Judicial Process: The United States Supreme Court's Use of Extra-Legal Materials in the Twentieth Century" (Unpublished Ph.D. Dissertation: University of Minnesota, 1974), pp. 241-244. This study was based upon a 10 percent random sample of all full opinions of the U.S. Supreme Court handed down in the 1925 through 1969 Terms of the Court.

3. Ibid., 243. The figures for the periods 1925-30 and 1961-70 were obtained by computing the mean averages of the different modes of legal construction for the several years in each period surveyed. For example, the 19.8 percent figure for common law-oriented Supreme Court cases in the 1920s is the mean of the totals for each Term of the Court analyzed in that period.

4. Richard J. Hoffman, "Classics in the Courts of the United States, 1790-1800," 22 *American Journal of Legal History* 55 (1978), passim.

5. Max Radin, "Sources of Law—New and Old," 1 *Southern California Law Review* 411, 412-413 (1928).

6. Ibid., passim.

7. *Corpus Juris Secundum* (St. Paul, 1936), I, v.

8. Ibid., v.

9. Martin Mayer, *The Lawyers* (New York, 1966), p. 420.

10. Radin, "Sources of Law—New and Old," 412-413, et passim.

11. John H. Wigmore, *A Treatise on the System of Evidence in Trials at Common Law*, 4 vols. (Boston, 1904-5).

12. Samuel Williston, *The Law of Contracts*, 4 vols. (New York, 1920).

13. Samuel Williston, *Life and Law* (Boston, 1940), pp. 264-265, Little Brown and Company. This poem is reprinted here in its entirety with the express permission of the publisher.

14. Ervin H. Pollack, *Fundamentals of Legal Research*, 3rd ed. (Brooklyn, 1967), pp. 115-116.

15. Williston, *Life and Law*, pp. 307-308.

16. "Report of the Special Committee Appointed to Consider and Report Whether the Present Delay and Uncertainty in Judicial Administration Can Be Lessened, and if so, By What Means," 8 *American Bar Association Reports* 323,329-331 (1885), cited in Nathan Crystal, "Codification and the Rise of the Restatement Movement" (Unpublished essay, 1978), 3.

17. On the American Law Institute and the Restatement, see William D. Lewis, "History of the American Law Institute and the First Restatement of the Law: How We Did It," in American Law Institute, ed., *Restatement*

in the Courts (St. Paul, 1945), pp. 1-23; Herbert F. Goodrich, "The Story of the American Law Institute," *Washington Law Quarterly* 283 (1951); and Crystal, "Codification and the Rise of the Restatement Movement."

18. American Law Institute, *Restatement of the Law of Contracts*, 2 vols. (St. Paul, 1932).

19. Goodrich, "The Story of the American Law Institute," 286.

20. Samuel Williston, "Written and Unwritten Law," 17 *American Bar Association Journal* 39, 41 (1931). The question of whether the Restatement was intended by its framers as a first step to a legal code is perceptively discussed in Crystal, "Codification and the Rise of the Restatement Movement," 17-20, et passim.

21. Thurman Arnold, *Symbols of Government* (New York, 1962), p. 51.

22. Goodrich, "The Story of the American Law Institute," 292.

23. Lewis, "How We Did It," p. 20.

24. Ibid., pp. 7-8.

25. In the 1930s, the restaters were subjected to a great deal of criticism for their excessive conceptualism. See Thurman Arnold, *Fair Fights and Foul* (New York, 1965), p. 58; Charles E. Clark, "Restatement of the Law of Contracts," 42 *Yale Law Journal* 643, 647 (1933). See also the recent criticisms of the Restatement in Lawrence M. Friedman, *A History of American Law* (New York, 1973), p. 582; Grant Gilmore, *The Ages of American Law* (New Haven, 1977), pp. 72-74; and Joel Seligman, *The High Citadel: The Influence of the Harvard Law School* (Boston, 1978), p. 46. See also the discussion of the realists' critiques of the Restatement, *infra*, chapter 7.

26. On the genesis and influence of the *Harvard Law Review*, see Charles Warren, *History of the Harvard Law School and of Early Legal Conditions in America* (New York, 1908), II, pp. 440-441; Williston, *Life and Law*, pp. 82-83; Friedman, pp. 547-548; and Seligman, pp. 40-41.

27. Ignore, for example, Samuel B. Clarke, "Criticisms upon Henry George, Reviewed from the Stand-Point of Justice," 1 *Harvard Law Review* 265 (1888); A. Lawrence Lowell, "The Responsibilities of American Lawyers," 1 *Harvard Law Review* 232 (1887); E. Irving Smith, "The Legal Aspects of the Southern Question," 2 *Harvard Law Review* 358 (1889).

28. 4 *Harvard Law Review* 193 (1890).

29. See, for example, "Lecture Notes: Contracts," 4 *Harvard Law Review* 39 (1890); "Lecture Notes: Evidence," 3 *Harvard Law Review* 332 (1890).

30. "Note," 1 *Harvard Law Review* 35, 35 (1887).

31. Quoted in Charles E. Hughes, "Forward," 50 *Yale Law Journal* 737, 737 (1941).

32. 244 U.S. 590, 606, 613, 615 (1917) (Brandeis, J., dissenting).

33. Chester A. Newland, "Innovation in Judicial Technique: The Brandeis Opinion," 42 *Southwestern Social Science Quarterly* 22, 25 (1961). Several of the justices appointed to the Court by President Franklin Roosevelt—Frankfurter, Douglas, and Black in particular—later surpassed Brandeis in the number and frequency of law review citations in their written opinions. Chester A. Newland, "Legal Periodicals and the United State Supreme Court," 3 *Midwest Journal of Political Science* 58, 62 (1959).

34. Chester A. Newland, "Comment: The Supreme Court and Legal Writing: Learned Journals or Vehicles of an Anti-Antitrust Lobby," 48 *Georgetown Law Journal* 105, 127 (1959).

35. 274 U.S. 357 (1927).

36. Charles Warren, "New Liberty under the Fourteenth Amendment," 39 *Harvard Law Review* 431 (1926).

37. 274 U.S. 357, 375-379 (1927) (Brandeis, J., dissenting).

38. Warren, "New Liberty under the Fourteenth Amendment," 460-465.

39. 283 U.S. 697 (1931).

40. Roscoe Pound, "Equitable Relief Against Defamation and Injuries to Personality," 29 *Harvard Law Review* 640 (1916). The article is cited at 283 U.S. 697, 716 (1931). On the influence of legal periodicals in *Whitney* v. *California* and *Near* v. *Minnesota*, see Paul L. Murphy, *The Meaning of Freedom of Speech: First Amendment Freedoms from Wilson to FDR* (Westport, Conn., 1972), pp. 264-265, 269-270, notes 369-371.

41. 304 U.S. 64 (1938).

42. 41 U.S. 1 (1842).

43. 304 U.S. 64, 72-77 (1938).

44. 37 *Harvard Law Review* 49 (1923).

45. 1 Stat. 73 (1789).

46. Warren, "New Light on the History of the Federal Judiciary Act of 1789," 51-52, et passim.

47. 304 U.S. 64, 72-73. See Newland, "Legal Periodicals and the United States Supreme Court," 66-68. In dissent, Justice Butler criticized Brandeis's reliance upon Warren's article. *Erie* v. *Tompkins*, 304 U.S. 64, 86 (1938) (Butler, J., dissenting).

48. Radin, "Sources of the Law—New and Old," 421.

49. Ibid., 418.

50. Benjamin Cardozo, "Introduction," in Committee of the Association of American Law Schools, ed., *Selected Readings on the Law of Contracts from American and English Periodicals* (New York, 1931), vii-xi.

51. Other justices have expressed similarly favorable views on the contribution of law reviews to judicial decision making. See, for instance,

Charles Evans Hughes, "Forward," 50 *Yale Law Journal* 737 (1941); Earl Warren, "Comment on the Fiftieth Anniversary of the *Northwestern University Law Review,"* 51 *Northwestern University Law Review* 1 (1956).

52. See Alpheus T. Mason, *William Howard Taft: Chief Justice* (New York, 1965), pp. 268-269.

53. Quoted in Murphy, p. 370, note 62.

54. Ibid.

55. See James Willard Hurst, *The Growth of American Law: The Law Makers* (Boston, 1950), pp. 256-294.

56. Two recent scholars have argued that the ABA and the AALS joined forces in the early twentieth century in an attempt to "cleanse" the bar, in effect conspiring to remove from the profession blacks, Jews, and recent immigrants and, thus, preserving the traditional hegemony at the bar of white, Anglo-Saxon Protestants. See Jerold Auerbach, "Enmity and Amity: Law Teachers and Practitioners, 1900-1922," 5 *Perspectives in American History* 551 (1971); Auerbach, *Unequal Justice: Lawyers and Social Change in Modern America* (New York, 1976), pp. 93-129; and William R. Johnson, *Schooled Lawyers: A Study in the Clash of Professional Cultures* (New York, 1978), pp. 148-153. Although Auerbach and Johnson clearly demonstrate that certain influential bar association leaders and law school deans held racist and nativist views, the conspiracy thesis they suggest is open to criticism. See esp. Stephen Botein, "Review Essay: Professional History Reconsidered," 21 *American Journal of Legal History* 60, 63, 69-77 (1977); and Paul L. Murphy, "Rev. of *Unequal Justice* by Jerold Auerbach," 64 *Journal of American History* 497 (1977).

57. William R. Johnson, xi, et passim.

58. Accounts of the formation of the law school professoriate in the early twentieth century include Auerbach, *Unequal Justice*, pp. 74-101; Robert Stevens, "Two Cheers for 1870: The American Law School," 5 *Perspectives in American History* 405, 430-441 (1971); Seligman, pp. 20-46; and William R. Johnson, pp. 120-179.

59. The phrase, "search for order" is suggested by Robert Wiebe's aptly titled book, *The Search for Order, 1877-1920* (New York, 1967). An early chapter of *The Search for Order* provides a good, general discussion of the stepped up organization and realignment of America's major professions—including the legal profession—in the early twentieth century. See Wiebe, pp. 111-132.

60. Christopher C. Langdell, *A Selection of Cases on the Law of Contracts* (Boston, 1871), iv.

61. For a good, brief discussion of the nature and early flowering of the case method, see Stevens, "Two Cheers for 1870," 435-441.

62. Lewis, "How We Did It," p. 1.

5
THE EMBRACE OF
LEGISLATIVE HISTORY

If the common law-orientation of the American legal community was partially supplanted by the new sources of information created in the early twentieth century, it was further diminished by the favorable judicial reception to a source of information that had been in existence since the founding of the republic. This category of information is usually termed "legislative history." Legislative history is a phrase with a double meaning. Commonly, it refers to the sequence of steps in the passage of a piece of legislation through Congress or the state legislatures. The other understanding of the term—the one that is germane here—relates to published materials having a bearing on the intentions of an elected body that passes a particular piece of legislation or proposes a constitutional amendment. Generally, legislative history is said to include committee reports, published legislative hearings, and the recorded debates of members of the elected bodies. For example, the legislative history of the Civil Rights Act of 1964[1] would include the published report of the Congressional committee that drafted the Law and the statements made by supporters of the bill on the floor of Congress during deliberation over its purposes and specific wording. The United States Government Printing Office has published various sources of Congressional legislative history since 1774.[2] However, only in this century have states shown much interest in publishing reports of their own legislative history.

Since appellate courts purport to be very interested in the "intentions of the framers" of statutes or constitutional amendments, it seems logical that they would frequently consult legislative history. Yet, from the establishment of constitutional government in 1789 until late in the nineteenth century, the country's appellate courts generally refused to consult legislative documents for any information on the intentions behind particular pieces of legislation.[3] A discussion of some of the reasons for the appellate judiciary's neglect of legislative history is in order before turning to an examination of the tremendous upsurge of judicial reliance upon the information contained in legislative documents in the twentieth century.

The Resistance to Legislative History as a Source of Information

The pre-twentieth-century penchant to ignore the expressed wishes of the people's elected representatives stemmed, in part, from the antagonism that common law jurists had long felt toward statutes and their authors. Edward Dumbauld, a former Federal District Judge himself, once voiced this disdain rather elegantly: "In the Anglo-American system . . . statutes are ordinarily regarded as isolated or sporadic encrustations upon the rationally developed body of the judge-made common law."[4] The distaste for statutes among nineteenth-century devotees of the common law was also, to some degree, a product of legal inertia—a powerful force, unquantifiable, but always present in any legal community. Past appellate judges and legal writers had long been suspicious of statutory encroachments into the domain of judge-made law. The greatest men in Anglo-American jurisprudence—Edward Coke, William Blackstone, James Kent, Joseph Story, and Oliver Wendell Holmes (at least in his early years)—had been champions of the common law. Blackstone, for example, in his *Commentaries on the Laws of England*,[5] conspicuously ignored the role of Parliament in his discourse on the laws of England. Moreover, when Holmes wrote in 1881 that the "life of the law has not been logic but experience,"[6] he was referring to the history of incremental changes in the judge-made common law, not to discontinuous statutory enactments.

The antilegislative mood of late nineteenth- and early twentieth-century American jurists also resulted from a sympathetic hearing for the special pleadings of a small group of conservative legal writers, headed by Thomas Cooley and Christopher Tiedeman. Cooley's *A Treatise on the Constitutional Limitations Which Rest Upon the Legislative Powers of the States of the American Union*,[7] published in 1868, and Tiedeman's *Treatise on the Limitations of the Police Power in the United States*,[8] published in 1886, were the most influential legal treatises of the late nineteenth century.[9] Both reflected, and perhaps influenced, the laissez-faire principles of appellate judges in the waning years of the century;[10] in addition, both posited arbitrary standards for judging the reasonableness of state legislation. Tiedeman's treatise was the more polemically laissez faire of the two. The following passages from its preface show the spirit of the work and help one grasp the motivation of its author.

Governmental interference is proclaimed and demanded everywhere as a sufficient panacea for every social evil which threatens the prosperity of society. Socialism, Communism, and Anarchism are rampant throughout the civilized world. The State is called on to protect the weak against the shrewdness of the stronger, to determine what wages a workingman shall receive for his labor. . . .

Contemplating these extra-ordinary demands of the great army of dis-contents, and their apparent power, with the growth and development of universal suffrage, to enforce their views of civil polity upon the civilized world, the conservative classes stand in constant fear of the advent of an absolution more tyranical and more unreasoning than any before experienced by man, the absolution of a democratic majority. . . .

If the author succeeds in any measure in his attempt to awaken the public mind to a full appreciation of the power of constitutional limitations to protect private rights against the radical experimentations of social reformers, he will feel that he has been amply requited for his labors in the course of social order and personal liberty.[11]

If the "radical experimentations of social reformers," ensconced in state legislatures and Congress, were to be resisted by the appellate bench, one way to do so was seen to be through a literalistic interpretation of remedial legislation such as the Granger Laws[12] and maximum-hours laws.[13] In practice, this often meant cleaving to the letter rather than the spirit of such laws and disregarding the purpose of the lawmakers by ignoring any available legislative history.

This truncated view of statutory interpretation was reinforced by two "canons," that is, guidelines for legislative construction, that had great popularity among appellate judges in the late nineteenth and early twentieth centuries: the "derogation canon" and the "plain meaning rule."[14] The derogation canon held simply that statutes in opposition to the common law were not to be extended by construction. This canon meant, in effect, that legislative change was to be given the narrowest possible sway in altering the judge-made law. The plain meaning rule decreed that the courts should not look past the exact language of a statute unless the words were *prima facie* confusing or lent themselves to absurd consequences when applied to particular situations at bar. Both canons operated, occasionally in tandem, to provide convenient legal rationales for courts to avoid the perusal of legislative history and, thus, to restrict the application of remedial legislation. An example of the limiting effect of each canon should illustrate these points.

Wisconsin was the pioneering state in the passage of workmen's compensation legislation in this country. However, its state supreme court used the derogation canon on several occasions in its interpretation of the state's laws to deny recovery to injured workingmen or their representatives. A section of a 1907 Wisconsin statute included this language: "Every railroad company . . . shall be liable for . . . damages . . . for all injuries whether resulting in death, or not, sustained by any of its employees. . . ."[15] Yet, in a 1911 case, the Wisconsin Supreme Court held that the words "Railroad company" in the 1907 Law were not meant to include an "electric interurban railway."[16] Thus, recovery was denied to the administratrix of a deceased employee of the electric railway company involved in the case. In the course of its opinion, the court enunciated the familiar derogation canon in somewhat effusive language: "Where a statute is drastic and its burden heavy it is not permissible to bring within its terms by latitudinous construction those not named therein."[17] Although the court did not have legislative committee reports or debates relating to the 1907 Law to draw upon, it did have, subject to judicial notice, the speeches of

Governor LaFollett and Governor Davidson, delivered to different sessions of the Wisconsin Assembly, regarding the need for broad remedial workmen's compensation laws. These speeches were transcribed in the state's *Assembly Journal*[18] and were presented to the appeals court in support of the administratrix's position. However, these pieces of testimony were ignored by the court. This case presents a classic example of how the thrust of a statute can be blunted by construction. The effect in the case was to deny recovery to the injured party's representative, but this was accomplished without striking down the law involved or unduly antagonizing the legislature. The attitude of the Wisconsin court in this case is similar to that of the "common law lawyer" who, according to Roscoe Pound, "can hardly conceive that a rule of statutory origin may be treated as a permanent part of the general body of the law."[19]

The U.S. Supreme Court case of *Caminetti* v. *U.S.*[20] illustrates the restrictive effect on the use of legislative history that could be achieved by application of the plain meaning rule. The Mann Act of 1910[21] made it a federal offense to aid in the transportation of a woman across a state line "for the purpose of prostitution or debauchery or for any other immoral purpose." The question in this 1917 case was whether this Act applied to the case of a young man who had driven a consenting young woman (both were over the age of majority) from California to Nevada, spending the night with her in a private room in Reno. The man admitted having intercourse with the woman, but it was found that no commercial element had entered into the "transaction." On appeal, the U.S. Supreme Court held that the words of the statute were "plain and unambiguous" and that the man's conduct fell within the statute's designation of "other immoral purpose."[22] The Court's majority ignored the information gleaned from legislative material presented by attorneys for the petitioner, attesting that the Mann Act was directed solely at the "interstate ramifications of commercial vice;"[23] the Act was even titled "The White Slave Traffic Act." Justice McKenna dissented vehemently, citing at length the legislative history of the Act.[24]

The turn-of-the-century appellate judiciary's frequent refusal to consult legislative history was further reinforced by the philosophy of legal education prominent at the time. As has been previously noted, the case method of Langdell and his pedagogical progeny maintained that all of the available materials of the "science" of the law were contained in printed books, primarily the reports of appellate court decisions.[25] Langdell believed the law was a self-sufficient system; its premises, he submitted, were formulated by lawyers, and its growth required only the logical development of the precedents laid down in the reported decisions. Langdell's first casebook on contracts, published in 1871, reflected these attitudes.[26] It was not until the late 1920s that American law students were able to study from texts that contained a substantial amount of legislative and other noncase authorities.[27] The case-trained lawyers and judges of the early twentieth century, thus, were not merely unconvinced of the need for reliance upon legislative history in statutory construction; they were also unprepared by training to take advantage of such authorities.

The Conversion to Legislative History

The first third of the twentieth century witnessed a much more pronounced use of legislative history in the interpretation of state and Congressional laws than was evidenced during the entire nineteenth century. Nevertheless, it is impossible to pinpoint an exact date at which, for example, the U.S. Supreme Court began to accept information gleaned from committee reports and legislative debates for use in establishing "legislative intent." In *Church of the Holy Trinity* v. *U.S.*,[28] a decision handed down in 1892 which construed a statute that prohibited individuals or organizations from assisting in the importation of aliens under contracts for services, the High Court used legislative history to conclude that Congress had not meant to prohibit a church from securing a well-educated minister from abroad and paying for his transportation to the United States. Drawing from a report of the Senate Committee on Education and Labor, the Court acknowledged the fact that Congress did not intend by this legislation to prevent professional groups from securing highly qualified personnel from abroad; rather, the purpose of the Act, as clearly revealed in a statement by the Committee, was to prevent large business enterprises from importing low-cost manual labor from overseas, thus depressing the wages for unskilled native workers.[29]

One constitutional scholar has claimed that the *Church of the Holy Trinity* case signaled the turning point for judicial reception of legislative history.[30] Yet, an 1897 opinion of the Court in *U.S.* v. *Trans-Missouri Freight Association*[31] included the statement that "debates in Congress are not appropriate sources of information from which to discover the meaning of the language of a statute passed by that body."[32] In that decision, the Court essentially took the nihilistic position that the only thing that can be deduced from Congressional debates is that different members of the body have different views.[33] Even as late as 1929, in *U.S.* v. *Missouri Pacific Railway*,[34] the Court expressed hesitation in sanctioning the use of legislative materials to decipher Congressional intentions. But the ambivalence of appellate courts in determining whether to rely upon information contained in legislative history is best expressed in this contradictory statement from the 1904 decision of *Binns* v. *U.S.*:

While it is generally true that debates in Congress are not appropriate sources of information from which to discover the meaning of the language of a statute passed by that body, . . . yet it is also true that we have examined the reports of the committees of either body with a view of determining the scope of statutes passed on the strength of such reports.[35]

Not surprisingly, the authorities for this muddled "principle" are the diverging holdings in *Church of the Holy Trinity* and *U.S.* v. *Trans-Missouri Freight Association*.

In spite of the Supreme Court's reluctance in the early twentieth century to endorse consistently the use of legislative history, majority opinions of the Court after 1890 cited legislative materials with greater and greater frequency.[36] Quantitative data from a sample of full-dress opinions of the U.S. Supreme Court indicate that, in the period 1925-30, legislative history was explicitly cited in an average of about 5 percent of the full opinions per Term; in the 1930s legislative history was directly alluded to in an average of almost 20 percent of the full opinions each Term. In fact, by the late 1930s, no other category of extra-legal information was cited so frequently by the U.S. Supreme Court. Still, today, Congressional documents are cited more regularly by the High Court than any other type of extra-legal source of information.[37] Therefore, in spite of the quibbles of someone like Justice Butler in his 1929 majority opinion in *U.S.* v. *Missouri Pacific Railway*,[38] it is probably safe to agree with James Willard Hurst that by 1930 "it was more or less explicitly recognized that almost any official sources contemporary with the passage of a statute might be used in its interpretation."[39] Moreover, it was in the early 1930s that lawyers and judges began speaking about an "American rule"—in contrast to a more restrictive "British rule"—that permitted the use of committee reports and explanations ventured by a bill's sponsor in that bill's judicial construction.[40]

It is one thing to chart, however inexactly, the rising appellate cognizance of legislative history in the early twentieth century; it is another matter to account for the shift from the nineteenth-century antipathy to the twentieth-century acceptance. Unfortunately, appellate judges of the period were not disposed to make references to this transition in their correspondence or memoirs. So the reasons for the growth of a favorable judicial reaction to legislative history have to be provided in an impressionistic fashion. It must also be acknowledged that some of the explanatory factors about to be suggested may be as much concomitant as causative. This is an unavoidable risk of intellectual-legal analysis.

There is one obvious reason for the appellate courts' increased reliance upon the information contained in legislative documents in the first third of the twentieth century. The sheer increase in the amount of statute-related litigation reaching the appellate courts, particularly the U.S. Supreme Court, made it all but inevitable that the courts would have to come to terms with a substantial amount of legislative history. Proper construction of a statute such as the Interstate Commerce Act of 1887,[41] which supplanted a good deal of the common law relating to common carriers, required that lawyers and appellate judges become conversant with the intentions of the legislators most intimately involved with the passage of the Act. Initially, use of such explanatory legislative history was resisted due to judicial inertia, the application of restrictive canons of statutory interpretation, the heavy hand of the case method, and other factors previously considererd. However, by about the time of World War I, legislative history was receiving a frequent and often exhaustive hearing by the appellate courts.

Clearly, the individual most responsible for sensitizing the Supreme Court to legislative history was Louis Brandeis. The role of "Brandeis briefs" in connection with the presentation of so-called "social science" evidence—essentially the testimony of medical and industrial experts gleaned from professional journals—has already been discussed. But another aspect of these information-laden documents needs to be considered. The Brandeis brief provided a convenient medium for the recitation of legislative history in cases involving statutory construction. Although the relevance of the social science evidence in the early Brandeis briefs was seen as dubious to contemporaries and has been found to be lacking in quality by modern scholars,[42] the use of information-packed legislative history in the briefs seemed to be more palatable to the American legal community. Henry Wolf Biklé, a Philadelphia lawyer who taught at the University of Pennsylvania Law School in the 1920s and was for many years counsel to the Pennsylvania Railroad, lauded Brandeis briefs as valuable vehicles for apprising courts of pertinent "legislative facts," particularly those buried in committee reports and Congressional debates.[43]

Besides providing appellate advocates with a device for alerting judges and justices to legislative history, once Brandeis assumed his seat on the Supreme Court he began to cite legislative history himself with ample frequency. Brandeis's dissent in the now familiar employment agency case, *Adams* v. *Tanner*,[44] not only contained references to law review articles and texts on labor law, but it also made copious mention of legislative documents such as the Report submitted to Congress by the Commission on Industrial Relations[45] and several reports of the state of Washington Bureau of Labor.[46] While the Court's majority refused to examine one shred of legislative evidence and, thus, struck down the state law that had banned employment agencies from operating in Washington, Brandeis took the logical step of looking directly into the motives of the legislators. He found that the Washington legislature had reviewed substantial evidence attesting to the extortionist practices of employment agencies. This documentation was contained in detailed legislative hearings and committee reports.[47]

After the *Adams* dissent, Brandeis continued to draw upon the information contained in legislative documents. His contribution to the legal community's eventually favorable reception of legisla-

tive history was both as an example and as an advocate. Between
1925 and his retirement from the Court in 1939, Brandeis cited
Congressional documents in 12.9 percent of his opinions and other
government documents in 16.1 percent of his opinions.[48] No justice
of Brandeis's vintage relied so heavily upon the information found
in legislative history. Only in the late thirties, well after the battle
over the permissible use of legislative history in the judicial process
had been won, did justices begin to cite legislative materials with
greater frequency than Brandeis had in the previous generation.[49]

It was also Brandeis's apology for the use of information contained in legislative documents that was of service to the American
legal community's new devotion to information in the twentieth
century. For example, dissenting in *Jay Burns Baking Company*
v. *Bryan*,[50] Brandeis argued that the wisdom of a Nebraska law
that prescribed minimum weights for loaves of bread could be
assessed only by looking at the legislative history underpinning the
Nebraska statute and similar statutes in other states. After including
pages of information on bread making and weights and measures
in his dissent—most of which was drawn from legislative materials—Brandeis stated:

Much evidence referred to by me is not in the record. . . . It is the history of
the experience gained under similar legislation. . . . Of such events in our
history . . . the Court should acquire knowledge, and must, in my opinion,
take judicial notice, whenever required to perform the delicate judicial
task here involved.[51]

Arguments such as this for the judicial use of information from
legislative materials found their way into a number of Brandeis's
famous opinions.[52]

Brandeis's crusade for greater judicial reliance upon legislative
history, directed from his seat on the Supreme Court bench, was
bolstered by a variety of individuals and groups outside of the court
system. As has been noted, pressure groups, such as the National
Consumers' League, helped finance, research, and organize cases
on appeal. Before his appointment to the Court, Brandeis was the
League's principal legal advisor, working closely with Josephine
Goldmark, Chairman of the League's Committee on Legislation.

The League was especially interested in defending state maximum-hours and minimum-wage laws. In the appellate briefs that the National Consumers' League helped draft for such cases, frequent references were made to legislative history. Undoubtedly, even more mention would have been made of information contained in legislative sources if more states at the time had seen fit to publish the committee reports and floor debates of their legislatures. In any case, the National Consumers' League helped compile fifteen major Supreme Court briefs relating to wage and hour cases between 1908 and 1936.[53] Besides helping to assemble the briefs, the League publicized the cause of state regulatory legislation by sending copies of its briefs to law schools, libraries, and important individuals.[54]

Another set of stimuli for the increasingly favorable reception to legislative history in the legal community came from the law schools. In 1914, under a grant from the Carnegie Foundation, a volume titled *The Common Law and the Case Method in American University Law Schools* was published. Compiled and written by Austrian scholar Josef Redlich,[55] a distinguished continental legal authority, the "Redlich Report," while largely lauding the case method of instruction, suggested that the leading American law schools would be well served by giving their students more legislative materials to study and fewer cases.[56] In 1921, also under the sponsorship of the Carnegie Foundation, an even more definitive study of legal education was published: *Training for the Public Profession of the Law*, compiled by American attorney, Alfred Z. Reed.[57] The "Reed Report" was much more scathing in its criticism of legal education than the 1914 Carnegie study. Like its predecessor, though, it too suggested that law schools incorporate more discussion of statutes and legislative history into their curricula.[58] Besides sparking a great deal of controversy and comment among legal educators,[59] the two Carnegie studies caused a few prestigious law schools to take hesitant steps toward the inclusion of legislative materials in their courses, thus resulting in the acquaintance of future lawyers and judges with the information contained in legislative history. The important changes in law school instruction that resulted from the introduction of legislative materials into the curricula are considered in conjunction with a general discussion of legal education in the interwar years in the following chapter.

Indexes of the Shifting Attitude toward Legislative History

In commenting on nineteenth-century changes in the common law, a noted legal historian observed that "in periods of great conceptual tension, there emerges a treatise writer who tries to smooth over existing stresses in the law."[60] In the early twentieth century, whether appellate courts would or should take official notice of information contained in legislative documents was one crucial dimension of tension among members of the American legal community. Ernst Freund, a professor of law at the University of Chicago, was the early twentieth-century legal writer most illustrative of this tension. In his two major publications, Freund evidenced very different reactions to legislative history, but he wrote as if the thinking behind his two volumes was part of one coherent whole.

In 1904 Freund published his first important legal treatise, *The Police Power, Public Policy and Constitutional Rights.*[61] In this volume he argued for the appellate use of some fairly arbitrary, virtually a priori standards by which to judge the constitutional validity of legislation. In the "Introduction" to *The Police Power*, Freund listed several questions that he maintained should be asked of every law purporting to be a remedial health or safety measure before such a law could be judged constitutional:

Does a danger exist? Is it of sufficient magnitude? Does it concern the public? Does the proposed measure tend to remove it? Is the restraint or requirement in proportion to the danger? Is it possible to secure the object sought without impairing initial rights, essential rights and principles? Does a choice of the particular measure show that some other interest than safety or health was the actual motive of the legislation?[62]

It is important to note that this set of questions was cited by counsel and alluded to generally in the 1905 majority opinion in *Lochner* v. *New York*,[63] the famous case in which the Supreme Court ruled New York's maximum-hours law for bakers unconstitutional. Neither Justice Peckham's opinion of the Court in *Lochner* nor Freund's 1904 text devoted much attention to the need for a perusal of legislative materials in appellate decision making. This is particularly illuminating because both *The Police Power* and Peckham's opinion speculated upon legislative motivation; yet neither stressed the need for any judicial examination of the legislative history of statutes. The *Lochner* majority and Freund (at least in his 1904 text) were less interested in what the state legislatures *said* than in what they *suspected* motivated the state legislatures. Holmes dissenting in *Lochner*, put the matter simply but cogently:

This case is decided upon an economic theory which a large part of the country does not entertain. . . . The decision [depends] on a judgment or intuition more subtle than any articulate major premise.[64]

The economic theory to which Holmes was alluding wase, of course, laissez-faire conservatism.[65]

In 1917 Freund published his other important treatise on statutory construction, *The Standards of American Legislation: An Estimate of Restrictive and Constructive Factors.*[66] Although Freund did not explicitly renounce the rather arbitrary postulates for statutory construction enunciated in 1904, the points he raised in his 1917 text revealed that his position had changed substantially regarding the way in which courts should scrutinize legislative enactments. For instance, he stated that the factual bases of legislation should be evaluated on only two grounds: (1) that factual conclusions should not be reached in the face of undisputed evidence to the contrary, and (2) that, in the absence of factual evidence, the assumed basis of legislation should not be opposed to understandings and beliefs so general and so strong that courts are compelled to take judicial notice of them.[67] Freund followed up this point with an expression of hope that some day courts would be able to "demand that a legislature only act upon some evidence, somewhere in the record. . . ."[68] This reads almost like a plea for lawmaking bodies to compile more complete legislative histories for the benefit of the courts.

In short, in just over a decade, Freund had moved from the position of an omniscient observer, setting out arbitrary standards for legislative validity to be enforced by the courts, to that of someone beseeching the legislatures to provide more careful records of what they are doing so the courts will not misinterpret their intentions or act without appropriate information. In the final pages of *The Standards of American Legislation*,[69] Freund discussed reasons for the failure of legislatures to provide reasonably grounded legislation and suggested ways in which lawmakers could draft better statutes. In this context, he strongly endorsed the need to manufacture and record better legislative histories to provide appellate courts with the information necessary to permit them to construe statutes properly. He noted that although legislative history might have been ample for some Congressional enactments, it was sadly lacking for most state laws. Freund left the distinct impression that the meager judicial reliance upon legislative history as late as 1917 was due more to incompetent and lazy legislators than to self-serving judges. Whether this theory has merit is subject to debate. In any event, the views expressed in Freund's 1917 treatise clearly represented a much more sympathetic attitude of the American legal community toward statutes and the information contained in legislative history than had been evident in the previous decade.

By 1930 the use of information drawn from legislative history for the purpose of statutory construction was well established. No longer was any significant argument apparent within the legal community over the *legitimacy* of using information elicited from committee reports and legislative proceedings to construe statutes. What disagreement that remained over the use of legislative materials had to do with the difficulties of *deciphering* legislative intent and determing the *degree* to which that intent should be binding on the courts. A spirited exchange between Max Radin and James M. Landis, in volume 43 of the *Harvard Law Review*,[70] illustrates these concerns. In his inimitable style, Radin submitted that legislative intent was "a queerly amorphous piece of slag," undiscoverable in fact and irrelevant if discovered.[71] He maintained that there was no such thing as a single legislative intent or purpose behind a given statute. Too many minds, he insisted, combined to draft the final version of a statute for a single intent to emerge unscathed by ambiguity. Radin's views on the infeasibility of discovering and implementing legislative purpose prefigured those of later commentators on statutory construction such as Felix Frankfurter[72] and Karl Llewellyn.[73] Yet, none of these authorities in any way denied the legitimacy of employing data taken from legislative materials in the interpretation of statutes. They merely stressed the primacy of the words of the enactment itself. In Frankfurter's terms, ". . . while courts are no longer confined to the language of a statute, they are still confined by it."[74]

In his exchange with Radin, James Landis, a prominent New Deal appointee and later dean of the Harvard Law School, expressed a much less cynical attitude toward the use of legislative history in discovering legislative intent. He concluded:

The assumption, that the meaning of a representative assembly attached to the words used in a particular statute is rarely discoverable, has little foundation in fact.[75]

Landis contended that the records of legislative assemblies, if read with a knowledge of legislative procedure, often revealed the richest kinds of evidence of the lawmakers' purposes. He argued that a careful study of committee reports and the explanation of committee chairmen, if favorably acted upon by an assembly, become, in effect, a concurrence of the views of many. From analysis such as this, Landis submitted that legislative intent was discoverable in most cases from the information contained in committee reports and transcribed debates.

It is doubtful that Landis's wholesale embrace of legislative history was typical of professional attitudes in the 1930s. It is also unlikely that Radin's opinion of legislative intent as a "queerly amorphous piece of slag" was shared by many of the practitioners and legal experts of the day. Most likely, the balance of judges and attorneys involved in appellate litigation in the 1930s held views on the utility of legislative history somewhere between the extreme positions manned by Landis and Radin. They were, in all probability, skeptical of the truths provided by committee reports and records of assembly debates, but not afraid or reluctant to cite information drawn from such sources in support of their particular contentions.

Notes

1. 78 Stat. 241 (1964).
2. Benjamin Poore, ed., *Descriptive Catalogue of the Government Publications of the United States, 1774-1881* (Washington, 1885), p. 1

3. Jacobus ten Broek, "Admissibility and Use by the United States Supreme Court of Extrinsic Aids in Constitutional Construction," 26 *California Law Review* 287, 307 (1938); and James Willard Hurst, *The Growth of American Law: The Law Makers* (Boston, 1950), pp. 187-189.

4. Edward Dumbauld, "Legal Records in English and American Courts," 36 *American Archivist* 15, 30 (1973).

5. William Blackstone, *Commentaries on the Laws of England*, George Chase, ed., 4 vols. (Boston, 1876).

6. Oliver Wendell Holmes, Jr., *The Common Law* (Boston, 1881), p. 1

7. (Boston, 1868).

8. (St. Louis, 1886).

9. See Clyde E. Jacobs, *Law Writers and the Courts: The Influence of Thomas M. Cooley, Christopher G. Tiedeman, and John F. Dillon Upon American Constitutional Law* (Berkeley, 1954), pp. 27, 58-59.

10. See Arnold Paul, *Conservative Crisis and the Rule of Law: Attitudes of Bar and Bench, 1887-1895* (New York, 1969), pp. 12-18, et passim. See also Jacobs, pp. 23-97. Cf. Alan Jones, "Thomas M. Cooley and 'Laissez-Faire Constitutionalism': A Reconsideration," 53 *Journal of American History* 759 (1967). For a treatment that suggests that lawyers had a particularly pronounced impact upon the laissez-faire decisions of appellate courts in the period, see Benjamin R. Twiss, *Lawyers and the Constitution: How Laissez Faire Came to the Supreme Court* (Princeton, 1942).

11. Christopher G. Tiedeman, *Treatise on the Limitations of the Police Power in the United States* (St. Louis, 1886), vi-viii.

12. The "Granger Laws" were statutes passed in the late nineteenth century, generally by western and midwestern states, that attempted to regulate railroad charges and crop storage fees. Their passage was advocated principally by loosely organized, farmer-dominated bodies called "Granges." The Granges were able to convince several state legislatures that the rates charged by railroads and public utilities for the transportation and storage of crops were set too high and, thus, needed to be regulated by statute. See Charles Fairman, "The So-Called Granger Cases, Lord Hale, and Justice Bradley," 5 *Stanford Law Review* 587 (1953); Harry Scheiber, "The Road to *Munn*: Eminent Domain and The Concept of Public Purpose in the State Courts," 5 *Perspectives in American History* 327 (1971); and Robert Hunt, *Law and Locomotives* (Madison, 1958). The landmark U.S. Supreme Court decision on the Granger Laws was *Munn* v. *Illinois*, 94 U.S. 113 (1877).

13. State laws establishing maximum hours for an individual's labor within particular industries were passed with great frequency between 1890 and 1920. See Clement Vose, *Constitutional Change: Amendment Politics*

and Supreme Court Litigation Since 1900 (Lexington, Mass., 1972), pp. 170-176; Ray Brown, "Police Power—Legislation for Health and Personal Safety," 42 *Harvard Law Review* 866 (1929); Felix Frankfurter, "Hours of Labor and Realism in Constitutional Law," 29 *Harvard Law Review* 353 (1916). The leading U.S. Supreme Court cases construing state maximum-hours law were *Bunting* v. *Oregon*, 243 U.S. 426 (1917); *Muller* v. *Oregon*, 208 U.S. 412 (1908); *Lochner* v. *New York*, 198 U.S. 45 (1905); and *Holden* v. *Hardy*, 169 U.S. 366 (1898).

14. See Harry Jones, "The Plain Meaning Rule and Extrinsic Aids in the Interpretation of Federal Statutes," 25 *Washington University Law Quarterly* 2 (1939). The classic article on statutory construction, illustrating the point that for every restrictive canon there exists a corresponding expansive canon, is Karl Llewellyn, "Remarks on the Theory of Appellate Decision and the Rules or Canons About How Statutes Are to Be Construed," 3 *Vanderbilt Law Review* 395 (1950). See also Felix Frankfurter, "Reflections on Reading Statutes," in Alan Westin, ed., *An Autobiography of the Supreme Court: Off-the-Bench Commentary By the Justices* (New York, 1963), p. 306

15. 1907 Wisconsin Laws, chapter 254, section 1816.

16. *Jones* v. *Milwaukee Electric Ry. & L. Company*, 147 Wis. 427 (1911).

17. Ibid., 433.

18. *Wisconsin Assembly Journal* (1905), pp. 82-83; *Wisconsin Assembly Journal* (1907), pp. 60-61.

19. Roscoe Pound, "Common Law and Legislation," 21 *Harvard Law Review* 383, 385 (1908).

20. 242 U.S. 470 (1917).

21. 36 Stat. 825 (1910).

22. 242 U.S. 470, 489-490 (1917).

23. Ibid., 472-482.

24. Ibid., 496-503 (McKenna and Clarke, JJ., White, C.J., dissenting).

25. See the Address of Christopher C. Langdell to the Meeting of the Harvard Law School Association, November 5, 1886. Quoted in Charles Warren, *History of the Harvard Law School and of Early Legal Conditions in America* (New York, 1908), II, p. 374. See also my discussion of this subject, *supra*, chapter 2.

26. Christopher C. Langdell, *A Selection of Cases on the Law of Contracts* (Boston, 1871), iv.

27. See Albert Ehrenzweig, "The American Casebook: 'Cases and Materials,' " 32 *Georgetown Law Journal* 224 (1944), and my discussion, *infra*, chapter 6.

28. 143 U.S. 457 (1892).

29. Ibid., 464-465.

30. Jones, "The Plain Meaning Rule and Extrinsic Aids in the Interpretation of Federal Statutes," 14-15.

31. 166 U.S. 290 (1897).

32. Ibid., 319.

33. Ibid., 316-321.

34. 278 U.S. 269, 278 (1929).

35. 194 U.S. 486, 495-496 (1904).

36. See, for example, *The Delaware*, 161 U.S. 459, 472-473 (1896); *Buttfield* v. *Stranahan*, 192 U.S. 470, 494-496 (1903); and *U.S.* v. *St. Paul, M.&M. Railway Co.*, 247 U.S. 310, 316-318 (1918).

37. John W. Johnson, "The Dimensions of Non-Legal Evidence in the American Judicial Process: The United States Supreme Court's Use of Extra-Legal Materials in the Twentieth Century" (Unpublished Ph.D. Dissertation: University of Minnesota, 1974), pp. 215-234.

38. 278 U.S. 269, 278-279 (1929).

39. Hurst, pp. 187-189.

40. Frederick Weiner, *Briefing and Arguing Federal Appeals* (Washington, 1967), pp. 170-175. See also Edward Dumbauld, "The Lawyer's Use of Historical Materials" (Unpublished paper delivered at the Annual Meeting of the Southern Historical Association, 1963).

41. 24 Stat. 379 (1887).

42. See the discussion of the weaknesses in the early Brandeis briefs, *supra*, chapter 7. See also Paul L. Rosen, *The Supreme Court and Social Science* (Urbana, Ill., 1972), pp. 84-87.

43. Henry W. Biklé, "Judicial Determination of Questions of Fact Affecting the Constitutional Validity of Legislative Action," 38 *Harvard Law Review* 6, 12-14 (1924).

44. 244 U.S. 590, 597 (1917) (Brandeis, J., dissenting).

45. Ibid., 602.

46. Ibid., 598, 610-613.

47. Ibid., 609-612.

48. John W. Johnson, "The Dimensions of Non-Legal Evidence in the American Judicial Process," 230.

49. Ibid., 230-231, et passim.

50. 264 U.S. 504, 518 (1924) (Brandeis & Holmes, J.J., dissenting).

51. Ibid., 533-534.

52. See the opinions cited in chapter 3, note 37, *supra*.

53. See generally National Consumers' League, *Thirty-Five Years of Crusading, 1899-1935* (New York, 1935).

54. Clement Vose, "The National Consumers' League and the Brandeis Brief," 1 *Midwest Journal of Political Science* 267, 288 (1962).

55. (New York, 1914).

56. Ibid., p. 35.

57. (New York, 1921).

58. Ibid., pp. 379-380.

59. See Robert Stevens, "Two Cheers for 1870: The American Law School," 5 *Perspectives in American History* 405, 441-453 (1971).

60. Morton Horwitz, *The Transformation of American Law, 1780-1860* (Cambridge, Mass., 1977), p. 38.

61. (Chicago, 1904).

62. Ibid., "Introduction."

63. 198 U.S. 45, 48-49, 52-65 (1905).

64. Ibid., 75-76 (Holmes, J., dissenting).

65. See Robert G. McCloskey, *The American Supreme Court* (Chicago, 1960), p. 154; and Alfred Kelly and Winfred Harbison, *The American Constitution: Its Origins and Development,* 4th ed. (New York, 1976), p. 496. In what was perhaps Holmes's most famous speech, "The Path of the Law," delivered at the dedication of a new building at the Boston University School of Law in 1897 when he was a member of the Supreme Judicial Court of Massachusetts, Holmes suggested what he believed was behind the conservative thinking of so many Americans around the turn of the century: "When socialism first began to be talked about, the comfortable classes of the community were a good deal frightened. I suspect that this fear has influenced judicial action. . . . [It] has led people who no longer hope to control the legislatures to look to the courts as expounders of the Constitutions, and that in some courts new principles have been discovered outside the bodies of those instruments. . . ." See "The Path of the Law" in Oliver Wendell Holmes, *Collected Legal Papers* (New York, 1920), pp. 167-202. That the justices comprising the *Lochner* majority entertained laissez-faire conservative beliefs privately was of little concern to Holmes. In fact, judging from the ideas expressed in some of Holmes's own off-the-bench speeches and writings, he too may well have accepted certain tenets of conservative social Darwinism. See, for example, *Collected Legal Papers*, pp. 279-282. Holmes was more disturbed by the majority's willingness to enshrine antigovernment, conservative, social Darwinist principles in constitutional law in opposition to the expressed wishes of the people's elected representatives. In the *Lochner* dissent, he put it this way: "If it were a question whether I agreed with that theory, I should desire to study it further and long before making up my mind. But I do not conceive that to be

my duty, because I strongly believe that my agreement or disagreement has nothing to do with the right of a majority to embody their opinions in law." 198 U.S. 45, 75 (1905). If this view had been found compelling by the Supreme Court's majority in 1905, little need would have existed for information-packed Brandeis briefs advising the justices of relevant legislative history. An acceptance of Holmes's view would have meant that neither lawyers nor appellate judges would have needed to examine legislative history to find data on the intentions of legislators. Holmes's own post-1905 Supreme Court opinions, consistent with the principle of tolerance expressed in his *Lochner* dissent, were seldom sprinkled with references to legislative materials or other extra-legal information. It is instructive to compare Holmes and the more information-oriented Louis Brandeis. Between 1916 and 1932, they were both associate justices on the Supreme Court. Brandeis was, of course, the man of facts and voluminous, extensively documented opinions. Holmes was more philosophical and concise, more prone to the felicitous epigram than the footnote. Yet, as is well-known, Holmes and Brandeis almost always voted together during their joint tenure on the High Court. See G. Edward White, *The American Judicial Tradition: Profiles of Leading American Judges* (New York, 1976), pp. 150-177. The elder justice frequently concurred in Brandeis's dissents and, perhaps even more remarkably, Holmes *never* dissented from one of Brandeis's majority opinions. Edward J. Bander, *Justice Holmes: Ex Cathedra* (Charlottesville, Va., 1966), xiv.

66. (Chicago, 1917).

67. Ibid., p. 99.

68. Ibid., p. 99.

69. Ibid., pp. 274-275.

70. Max Radin, "Statutory Interpretation," 43 *Harvard Law Review* 863 (1930); James M. Landis, "A Note on 'Statutory Interpretation,'" 43 *Harvard Law Review* 886 (1930).

71. Radin, "Statutory Interpretation," 872.

72. "I should say that the troublesome phase of construction is the determination of the extent to which extraneous documentation and external circumstances may be allowed to infiltrate the text on the theory that they were part of it, written in ink discernable to the judicial eye." Frankfurter, "Reflections on Reading Statutes," p. 308.

73. Llewellyn, "Remarks on the Theory of Appellate Decision," passim.

74. Frankfurter, "Reflections on Reading Statutes," p. 322.

75. Landis, "A Note on 'Statutory Interpretation,'" 888-889.

6
THE FERMENT IN AMERICAN LEGAL EDUCATION

When the case method of legal education was just gaining a toehold in the Harvard Law School curriculum in the 1870s and 1880s, few observers of American legal culture would have guessed at its staying power. Since the case method is, in its essentials at least, still being employed extensively by the country's major law schools, it is fair to describe this innovation of Christopher Langdell as the most important single contribution to American legal education.[1] Yet, beginning in the 1920s and carrying over into the next decade, the case method was subjected to probing and often vicious criticism from within the law schools themselves. Moreover, in the interwar years, two well-established law schools and one newly created institution for legal scholars adopted curricular reforms that provided what then seemed to be attractive pedagogical alternatives to the case method. Both the critiques of the case method and the enacted alternatives were, in large part, influenced by the informational mind-set of the period. Even though these challenges to the case method's hegemony in the law schools were subdued by the time of World War II, the intellectual excitement in legal education in the 1920s and 1930s provides yet another glimpse of the penchant for information at work.

The Carnegie Foundation Studies of Legal Education

Orthodoxy in employing the case method requires exclusive scrutiny of the reports of appellate court cases. The first searching examination of the case method—*The Common Law and the Case Method in American University Law Schools*, assembled by the Austrian scholar Josef Redlich in 1914[2]—found the case method to be a superior device for imparting an understanding of the nuances of a common law system. After investigating the use of the case method at ten leading American law schools, Redlich came away with a generally positive view of this pedagogical approach. In his words, the American law school employing the case method was "superior to any other institution in the world as a medium of preparation for the bar."[3]

Nevertheless, the Redlich Report ventured some telling criticisms of the case method. For one thing, it maintained that the case method gave short shrift to statutes and legislative materials.[4] Thus, just as leadership in the law was passing from the courts to the legislatures, the case method was serving to retard future lawyers' cognizance of this important transition. Moreover, the report noted that professors' preparation for case-method classes required an enormous expenditure of time. Consequently, devotees of the case method did not have as much time as lecturers to spend on original legal research and publication.[5] These criticisms were coupled with Redlich's observation that the study of cases seemed to function best when performed in conjunction with a study of general legal textbooks.[6] In essence, Redlich was saying that case study was a useful but by no means universal approach to an understanding of the law. Redlich called for greater use by law professors of statutory material, increased reliance upon general legal texts, and more devotion to the production of helpful treatises. He was arguing for a professoriate more able and willing to rely upon information outside of the reported cases in the training of young lawyers. The Redlich Report was widely read by members of the legal profession, and it drew substantial comment.[7]

Many of the criticisms of the Redlich Report were echoed by the second of the Carnegie Foundation studies on Legal education, *Training for the Public Profession of the Law*, published in 1921 under the supervision of a then little-known American lawyer,

Alfred Zantsinger Reed.[8] The Reed Report was more definitive in its commentary on American legal education than the Redlich Report. Although the author of the earlier report had based his judgments upon brief stays at a handful of leading eastern law schools, Alfred Reed, assisted by a large staff, had engaged in substantial research on the history of formal American legal education since the eighteenth century and had spent years investigating the contemporary status of legal instruction from the lowliest night law school to the pinnacle of the Harvard Law School. Like Redlich, Reed attacked American law schools for their virtual neglect of statutory law and legislative materials[9] and for their institutional bias against scholarship.[10] He also lamented that most law schools failed to provide adequate practical instruction for future attorneys[11] and decried what he saw as a "caste system" within the country's legal profession.[12]

There was another point raised by the Reed Report that reverberated in American legal circles throughout the next two decades and served to fuel the movement toward greater acknowledgment of extra-legal information by the country's legal community. The report maintained—much to the embarrassment of law school deans and professors—that the American law school curriculum was, even at its best, terribly unsystematic. As Reed put it:

No feature of American legal education so arouses the astonishment of a layman, or a foreign student familiar with the neat categories of Continental law, as does the absence of anything like agreement between our various law schools as how the law is to be divided and arranged; unless it be the further discovery that no single school has devised its curriculum upon any reasoned plan.[13]

Seen in the cold light of Reed's empirical investigation, American legal education in the early twenties was, then, by no means as scientific as Langdell had once so confidently maintained. It was out of a desire to rectify the chaotic state of American legal education so carefully exposed by the Reed Report that a series of important reforms in law school curricula—reforms that included substantial doses of extra-legal information—were initiated. These curricular changes did not all occur immediately as a direct result of the criticisms of the Redlich and Reed reports. Rather, in retrospect, it appears that the two Carnegie Foundation studies were simply the first links in a chain of events that threatened, for a time, to transform legal education permanently. The other links in this chain can now be examined in sequence.

Columbia Law School's "Functional Curriculum"

The range of undergraduate courses offered by the Law School of Columbia University at the close of World War I was fairly conventional. Most of the courses in the curriculum were of ancient lineage, the titles and general subject matter having been established to correspond with the headings of textbooks or encyclopedias.[14] But in the 1922-23 academic year, two novel courses appeared in the compulsory program for third year students: "Industrial Relations," taught by Noel Dowling; and "Illegal Combinations" (later called "Trade Regulations"), offered by Herman Oliphant. These two courses were to legal educators at Columbia in the 1920s as Langdell's course on contract law was to legal education at Harvard in the 1870s.[15] They served as the opening wedges in a major movement to revamp totally an institution's legal curriculum. The changes generated by these courses were soon to place Columbia at the forefront of the resistance to Harvard's case method.

The courses offered by Dowling and Oliphant were distinguished from the usual case method courses in several important respects. First, the materials for study were organized under the rubrics of social and economic problems rather than according to narrow legal categories. In short, in designing these courses, Oliphant and Dowling were reflecting their belief that legal study could not be confined by arbitrary boundaries. The Industrial Relations course employed textual material derived from contracts, torts, equity, agency, and constitutional law. The Trade Relations course drew upon the fields of contracts, torts, equity, criminal law, and corporations. Second, both courses used some "non-legal" materials. For example, the casebook[16] devised by Oliphant for the students in his Trade Regulations course opened with thirty-three pages of economic history and referred to several recent empirical studies by sociologists and economists. Finally, statutory materials were relied upon in both courses to an unprecedented degree. Harlan Fiske Stone, who was dean of the Columbia Law School when the courses by Oliphant and Dowling were adopted, later expressed his view on statutory material that was undoubtedly shared by his two innovative professors. Statutes and statutory materials, he maintained, are not "alien intruder[s] in the house of the common law, but . . . guest[s] to be welcomed and made at home there as . . . new and powerful aid[s] in the accomplishment of [their] appointed task of accommodating the law to social needs."[17]

The 1922-23 courses of Dowling and Oliphant were so well received by the Law School's faculty and students that by 1926 the idea was seriously entertained of reorganizing the entire three-year course of legal study around "functional courses" modeled after Trade Regulations and Industrial Relations. Those professors who looked with favor upon the two innovative courses argued that law students should be given a substantial exposure to how the law operated in a social context; they also agreed with Dowling and Oliphant that proper training in law required some grasp of how law was related to the social sciences. William O. Douglas, who became one of the leading advocates of the new curriculum after joining the Columbia law faculty in 1926, provided some insight into what motivated the Columbia reformers and what they hoped to accomplish:

We wanted interdepartmental fertilization of ideas—a process that critics later dubbed interdepartmental "sterilization" of ideas. In finance, we wanted to teach the anatomy of finance as well as the rules of law. In criminal law, we wanted psychiatry as well as the criminal code. In credit transactions, we wanted to explore all the institutions of credit as well as the commercial code. . . . If we could integrate the various disciplines, we could learn what the law should be, by learning the problems with which it must deal.[18]

Besides Oliphant, Dowling, and Douglas, the Columbia reformers included law professors Underhill Moore, Hessel Yntema, Karl Llewellyn, and Walter Wheeler Cook. All of these men later became identified prominently with the "legal realist movement." Also joining their ranks were Julius Goebel of Columbia's History Department and Thomas Reed Powell of Political Science. In 1926 committees from the faculty were appointed and charged with designing functional courses in each of the following areas: labor, finance and credit, business units, marketing, risk and risk bearing, criminal law, legal administration, family and familial property, legislation, and historical and comparative jurisprudence. The committees submitted to the faculty over eight hundred pages, describing their inquiries and making numerous recommendations about the design of functional courses. A recent scholar termed the Columbia study of legal education in the 1920s "the most comprehensive and searching investigation of law school objectives and methods that has ever been undertaken."[19]

In 1928, Herman Oliphant, a man Douglas described as "one of [the] . . . more acid tongued members" of the reforming cadres,[20] condensed the findings of the ten committees into a 195-page book, inelegantly titled *Summary of Studies in Legal Education by the Faculty of Columbia University*.[21] The *Summary* is remarkable for its specific suggestions on legal curricula—some of which are still meritorious. Given the composition of the committees—largely those members of the law faculty on record before 1926 as being in support of functional courses[22]—and the selection of Oliphant as the editor for the final document, it is not surprising that the *Summary* strongly endorsed the complete adoption of a functional curriculum. So in 1928 the Columbia Law School committed its energies and finances to a curriculum that had as its raison d' être an embrace of extra-legal information. Some of the new courses devised were: Landlord and Tenant, Trial Practice, Business Organization, Corporate Finance, Evidence, Legal History, Legislation, Comparative Law, Administrative Law, and even Accounting. The textual materials manufactured by the Columbia professors to use in these courses drew extensively from legislative history and the fields of business administration, economics, sociology, psychology, and history. Herbert Wechsler, a law student at Columbia between 1928 and 1931, referred to the efforts of his Columbia professors as raising "a frontal challenge to the concept of the common law as a closed legal system, yielding answers to all questions by conformity to earlier decisions or deductions from the principles that they declared."[23]

In spite of the energy and excitement generated by the Columbia functional curriculum in the late 1920s, the goal of integrating information successfully from the social sciences into legal education was temporarily sidetracked. The 1926-28 study of the wisdom of adopting a functional curriculum precipitated a conflict within the Columbia faculty over the purposes of a legal education. The leading advocates of a functionally oriented curriculum—Oliphant, Moore, Douglas, Yntema, and Cook—tended to think of themselves as a community of scholars, examining the law as an aspect of social organization and working with social scientists to assemble and sort through empirical data. Not surprisingly, their views clashed with the balance of the faculty, which saw the production of high-quality practicing lawyers as its principal duty.[24] When this latter faction eventually held sway, some of the apostles of the new curriculum resigned their professorships and went elsewhere to conduct their empirical inquiries and to draw upon the information compiled by social scientists.

The Columbia experiment also floundered because the contributions expected of the social sciences were not forthcoming. As one legal historian put it, "the social sciences had been oversold."[25] The initial enthusiasm over the social sciences at Columbia was not sustained. The suggestions of the social science consultants, which in the 1926-28 planning stages of the functional curriculum had seemed so pithy, did not offer much of substance when the professors "got down to cases." For instance, in 1934 Robert Hutchins reflected upon his disappointments with social science information. Hutchins, then president of the University of Chicago, had been the youngish dean of Yale's Law School between 1927 and 1929 and a supporter of the efforts of the Columbia reformers. According to Hutchins:

With the enthusiasm of converts they [social scientists] showed us the masses of social, political, economic and psychological data which lay hidden in the cases. . . . The fact was that though the social scientists seemed to have a great deal of information, we could not see and they could not tell us how to use it. It did not seem to show us what the courts would do or whether what they would do was right.[26]

To support this generalization, Hutchins alluded to the negligible contributions of psychology to the law of evidence, submitting that this social science offered little insight—despite engaging in much inquiry—into the question of what and how evidence affected juries.[27] Much harsher judgments on the failure of integrating social science information into legal education came from professors not nearly as sympathetic to the Columbia experiment as Hutchins. For example, Roscoe Pound, the dean of the Harvard Law School from 1916 to 1936, thought that courses such as those adopted at the Columbia Law School were "pretentious" in their emphasis on "so-called research" by the students themselves.[28]

Finally, it must be acknowledged that personalities and academic politics may have helped to sound the death knell for Columbia's functional curriculum. William Douglas claimed that the opposition of Columbia University President Nicholas Murray Butler to the curricular reforms led to the schism in the faculty that caused Yntema, Moore, Cook, Oliphant, and Douglas himself to leave Columbia.[29] President Butler, whom Douglas and his like-minded colleagues dubbed "Nicholas Miraculous" because of his intellectual arrogance, had originally given some support to Oliphant and the functionalists. However, when Dean Huger W. Jervey resigned because of ill health in early 1928 and Butler, without consulting the law faculty, appointed Young B. Smith, an old-guard law professor, as dean, a bitter debate within the faculty ensued. The curricular reformers had championed Oliphant for the deanship. In the aftermath of Butler's ill-advised appointment, the reformers sought to organize some form of protest, hoping to check Smith's installation as the new dean. Butler ignored their efforts. Although unsuccessful in countering the president's decision, the functionalists' charges led to a heated debate within the law faculty that all but destroyed the tenuous compromises that had been agreed to in inaugurating the new curriculum. Within two years, all of the leading advocates of empirical legal research at Columbia had resigned. Regardless of the reasons for the demise of Columbia's functional curriculum, the movement toward greater use of social science information in legal instruction and legal research was by no means at an end in 1928. The legal professoriate's flirtation with social science information continued for at least a decade, principally at the Johns Hopkins University Institute of Law and Yale University's Law School.

Empirical Legal Research at Johns Hopkins and Yale

Besides hoping to give their law students a more wholistic picture of society, the Columbia reformers were interested in expanding the horizons of legal research. After the schism at Columbia
occurred, several of the professors looked elsewhere for a congenial
scholarly community. One locale that drew the research-minded
members of the professoriate was the newly established Johns
Hopkins Institute of Law; the other was the Yale Law School.

The Institute of Law was founded in 1928 in Baltimore. Oliphant
and Yntema, who had resigned from the Columbia law faculty a
few months earlier, joined Walter Wheeler Cook and business
professor Leon Marshall as the leading scholars at the new Institute.
The Institute was a legal think tank; not by any stretch of the ima-
gination was it conceived of as a law school. According to Walter
Cook, the Institute had as its primary purpose the "non-profes-
sional study of law."[30] Before the founding of the Institute, almost
no statistics were available on judicial administration.[31] Therefore,
the Institute set as one of its first tasks the "development of large
masses of dependable data."[32] In cooperation with the judicial
councils of two states—Ohio and Maryland—the Institute sought
to accumulate data on the administration of justice in the state
court systems. In addition, it also began a survey on the range of
litigation in New York City civil actions. One of the book-length
studies turned out by the Institute, which produced some of the
longed-for statistics, was titled *Unlocking the Treasuries of the
Trial Courts*, authored by Leon Marshall and a group of associates.[33]
If this book did nothing else, it indicated to members of the Institute
and to any interested readers just how immense was the volume of
judicial business in America. The study reported a yearly total of
about three hundred thousand divorce cases alone, but it could
only speculate about the "millions upon millions" of criminal
actions in all the country's courts.[34] Rather than stopping to analyze
the information assembled in studies such as *Unlocking the Treasuries of the Trial Courts*, the members of the Institute plunged
ahead to gather more and more information. According to Marshall, who was perhaps the driving force behind the Institute's data

gathering, the researchers at Johns Hopkins hoped some day to establish a "permanent system of judicial records and statistics" that would provide information on matters such as the trends of litigation and delay in the courts.[35]

In 1933 the foundation money, upon which the Institute sorely depended, ran out, and the Institute of Law became another casualty of Depression-induced economics. Perhaps, if the Institute had survived longer, the members eventually would have found the time and energy to make some sense out of the mountains of data they had assembled. In any case, those publications that did spring from the work of the Institute were disappointing. For an organization that asked to be evaluated by the legal community on the basis of its publications,[36] the crudely empirical offerings were seen by some critics and even some sympathizers as an embarrassment to the field of legal research. One commentator on the labors of the Institute concluded that "its scientific work . . . reached approximately the same stage as Botany would, had its efforts been wholly devoted to counting leaves on trees."[37]

While Oliphant and Yntema turned south from Columbia in 1928, William O. Douglas and Underhill Moore headed northeast. Under the "boy dean," twenty-eight-year-old Robert Hutchins, the Yale Law School became the other center for empirical legal research in the interwar years. In conjunction with Yale's newly created Institute of Human Relations, a number of professors at the Law School began to engage in detailed legal research similar to that undertaken at the Johns Hopkins Institute.[38] When Hutchins left Yale for the presidency of the University of Chicago, Charles Clark became the Law School dean and continued to champion empirical legal research. Besides Hutchins and Clark, the most active proponents of data gathering in the Law School were the former Columbia rebels Underhill Moore and William O. Douglas. Along with a shifting pool of junior colleagues and research assistants, Clark, Moore, and Douglas published a series of law review articles in the 1930s that grew out of substantial quantitative research. Most of the articles appeared in the *Yale Law Journal*,[39] making this periodical the most significant expositor of the informational penchant in American legal culture in the period.

Dean Clark's work involved collecting and analyzing data on court administration in Connecticut. Besides bringing together data on civil and criminal cases for the purpose of describing the range of judicial business in the jurisdiction of a populous state, Clark focused on—among other things—jury trials. From his assembled statistics, Clark found that of all civil cases that terminated with some form of judicial action between 1919 and 1932, jury trials took place only about 7 percent of the time. Yet, Clark's information also disclosed that most of those trials involved automobile accident suits claiming negligence[40]—extremely costly and time-consuming affairs.[41] Clark's research into jury trials proved that if compensation for injuries and damages suffered in automobile accidents could be removed from the court dockets and administered by a tribunal without regard to fault, the number and the resulting inconvenience of jury trials would be almost eliminated. Hence, Clark's study provided some early fuel for the still continuing debate over the desirability of no-fault automobile insurance.

William Douglas, his collaborators, and his assistants worked diligently between 1928 and 1934 to ferret out information on the timely subject of bankruptcies. In the early stages of the Depression, when hundreds of businesses were forced to close each year, it was considered very important by researchers and policy makers alike to determine what situations led to business failures. The principal problem that Douglas faced was in the collection of information. The public documents from bankruptcy proceedings did not offer sufficient insights into the economic statuses of the businesses that failed or the characters of the individual businessmen to permit any warranted generalizations about what causes bankruptcies. So Douglas, Dorothy Thomas of the Institute for Human Relations, and a few other associates proceeded to do their own interviewing. For a time, Federal Judge William Clark even cooperated with Douglas by permitting the Yale researchers to use his courtroom to interview each bankrupt after he passed through the normal legal channels of the bankruptcy action. However, the bankruptcy "clinic" in the obliging federal court was forced to close for "political reasons" after querying only fifty-eight informants. Personal interviews continued elsewhere, and the Douglas

team of researchers secured other necessary information via mailed
questionnaires. After publishing two articles describing the method-
ological problems that beset this study,[42] Douglas began publishing
his substantive findings in 1932.[43] Undoubtedly Douglas's dedicated
research into the causes of business failures had something to do
with his appointment by President Roosevelt to the Securities and
Exchange Commission in 1936.[44]

The most ambitious and, at the same time, curious statistical
research engaged in at Yale was spearheaded by Underhill Moore.
Regarded as a stimulating and uncompromising teacher,[45] Moore
came to Yale from Columbia in 1929. His early research was founded upon the working hypothesis that given court decisions were
more directly caused by patterns of behavior within the jurisdictional areas from which they arise than upon the taught tradition of
the law. He called this the "institutional method."[46] In essence,
Moore believed that the cultural environments of accused criminals
and litigants determined their behavior and the resulting legal decisions that concerned them more than did legal precedents. Moore
set out to document this hypothesis by means of extremely meti-
culous research into subjects many other scholars considered trivial.[47]

His first such study at Yale involved a small point in the practice
of banking.[48] Assume a bank customer has borrowed money from
a bank on time. Can the bank, on the day the note matures, deduct
the amount due from the customer's account at the bank—without
notice to the customer—and, thus, fail to honor checks drawn by
the customer in excess of the remaining balance in the account?
When Moore began his search to answer this question, he found
that there were only three appellate court decisions included in all
of the court reports that addressed this specific question. The first
case, a 1904 South Carolina decision,[49] held that the bank's "setoff" was unjustified without prior notice to the customer. The
second and third cases, from New York and Pennsylvania respect-
ively,[50] held that a bank is within its rights to setoff the amount
owed against the customer's account without notice. Exhaustive
research into the court records did not reveal any factors that distinguished the South Carolina case from the New York and Pennsylvania cases. Moore, thus, concluded that the "legal method" of
analysis was "hopelessly inadequate."[51] Moore then investigated

bank practices on debiting accounts in several banks in each of the three jurisdictions at the approximate time each case arose. In addition, he surveyed the practices in his home state of Connecticut. From this research, which he tabulated carefully,[52] Moore found that, in the South Carolina, New York, and Pennsylvania cases, the bank behavior involved in the litigated cases deviated from the general banking practices at the time in their respective jurisdictions. However, in the South Carolina case, the bank's behavior flew more strongly in the face of prevailing cultural conventions than in the Pennsylvania and New York cases. So Moore concluded that the unacknowledged and probably unconscious standard employed by the courts in these cases was the degree of departure from institutional practices.[53] Moore and his associates employed this data-centered institutional method in other studies of banking behavior in the 1930s.[54]

In 1933 Moore embarked upon his most rigorous and time-consuming inquiry: a study of the behavior of individuals who drove and parked automobiles in an area bordering the Yale University campus in New Haven, Connecticut. Moore was particularly interested in determining whether groups of individuals drove and parked differently after the institution of specific ordinances regulating the operation and parking of automobiles. His analysis of New Haven drivers was not based upon his earlier developed institutional method, but upon certain postulates of the psychological "theory of learning." Moore conducted his field research on this project between 1933 and 1937 in collaboration with Charles Callahan, a researcher at Yale's Institute of Human Relations. Their master work, a 136-page law review article titled "Law and Learning Theory: A Study in Legal Control,"[55] was not published until 1943. This article is replete with tables, graphs, diagrams, and the jargon of behavioristic psychology. Karl Llewellyn probably had this article foremost in mind when he wrote in 1960 that Underhill Moore was the only legal scholar of the 1930s who "put forward his thinking as sufficiently complete to deserve description as a philosophy. . . ."[56]

As impressive as Moore's research and behavioral analysis clearly were, the image of this bald, bespectacled law professor, fitted out in Bermuda shorts and perched on a campstool beside a New Haven street noting the comings and goings of automobiles, is a bit humorous. In his memorial article on Moore, Charles Clark, an old friend and colleague of Moore's at Yale, relates a typically revealing anecdote from the days of the automobile study. According to Clark, one day while Moore was conducting his field research, he was greeted by an old friend outside the Taft Hotel in downtown New Haven. Moore, a usually affable man, was so engrossed in his data collection that he was reported to have glanced at the man only briefly, and said, "Don't bother me. Can't you see I'm busy counting these cars?"[57]

With Moore's "institutional method" and his "law and learning theory," the penchant for information was indulged to its fullest. None of the legal scholars of the interwar years matched Moore's capacity for field research. Moreover, no other legal scholar of the period had Moore's sophisticated grasp of social science methodology. A colleague and sympathetic critic, F.S.C. Northrop, stated shortly after Moore's death that the scholarship of Underhill Moore "probably marks not merely the culmination of the jurisprudence of the recent past but also a turning point in legal science generally."[58]

Although the empirical research at the Yale Law School did not come to as abrupt a halt as did the research at the Johns Hopkins Institute, it was clear that by the late 1930s the momentum for data collection had slowed in New Haven. The Institute for Human Relations continued to fund social science research, but less money was available to support the projects of law school professors.[59] In addition, two of the leading practitioners of empirical research left Yale for high-level government positions before the end of the decade: Douglas went to the Securities and Exchange Commission staff in 1934, to the Commission itself in 1936, and finally to the U.S. Supreme Court in 1939; and Clark was appointed as a circuit judge on the U.S. Court of Appeals, Second Circuit, in 1939. This left on the Yale Law School faculty only Underhill Moore as a leading apologist for and exemplar of empirical legal research.[60]

Meanwhile, Back at Harvard

To a degree, the informational fixation that was so manifested by law professors in the 1920s and 1930s at Columbia, the Institute of Law, and Yale was a reaction to the case method of instruction so frequently identified with the Harvard Law School. What the Columbia reformers and the empirical researchers at Johns Hopkins and Yale objected to in the case method was its essential closure. Langdell had asserted in an 1886 speech that the law is a science and that virtually all a student needs to know about the law can be found in the appellate court reports.[61] To this view, the curricular reformers and the empirical researchers of the 1920s and 1930s dissented strongly. They took it upon themselves to search for information and insights outside of the reported cases. The Columbia reformers were led to establish their functional courses, drawing in large part from statutory materials and other extra-legal sources; the members of the Institute of Law set to work gathering quantitative information on judicial administration; and a number of Yale law professors engaged in empirical research and, with the help of social scientists from the Institute of Human Relations, provided training in behavioral methodology to small classes of law students and graduate students.

While attempting to build their own new curriculum in conjunction with the social scientists, several Yale law professors heaped scorn upon Harvard's vaunted case method. Douglas, for instance, in an address to the American Association of College Schools of Business, blasted Harvard and the Langdell system for their inability to deal with the pressures brought to bear upon the law by the Depression. He argued that legal instruction that relied upon appellate court cases was, almost by definition, a generation behind social reality. He urged further that a fusion of law and the social sciences should be made a prominent goal of legal educators.[62]

The Harvard Law School faculty in the twenties and early thirties engaged in few dalliances with the social sciences. Under Dean Roscoe Pound, no important changes were made in the undergraduate curiculum of the Law School.[63] Pound, it was said by a member of the law faculty, ran the Law School like a business in which he was the majority shareholder.[64] Although Pound did help to raise money for graduate training in legal research at Harvard, he believed that the basic legal education that the Law School offered was more than satisfactory. He frequently pointed with pride at the successes of former students of the Law School in big-city law firms. In spite of faculty reports expressing some support for the innovations in legal instruction at Columbia and Yale, the Pound-led Harvard Law School continued to emphasize the teaching of the common law by means of the case method. Only after Pound retired as dean in 1936 did the Law School adopt noncommon law courses such as "Techniques of Regulation," "Business Enterprise," and "Government Litigation."[65] While law professors at Columbia, Johns Hopkins, and Yale were attempting to cross-pollinate law and the social sciences, many of the most distinguished Harvard professors were hard at work trying to purify the conventional strains of the common law. In the academic year 1929-30 alone, over one-quarter of the members of the Harvard Law School faculty were involved as reporters or advisors for the American Law Institute's Restatement.[66] Pound gave great encouragement to the work of the Restaters at Harvard, lauding their attempt to make the Harvard Law School the country's unofficial "ministry of justice."[67] Thurman Arnold, a Yale law professor and one of the most vocal critics of the work of the Restaters and the case method, referred to Harvard Law School in this period as the "high church of abstract legal theology."[68]

Although work for the American Law Institute's Restatement was clearly the most notable research performed by the Harvard law faculty in the 1920s and 1930s, at least three Harvard law professors engaged in empirical studies. As the aftermath of a major scandal in Cleveland, Ohio, in which a municipal court judge was accused of second degree murder, Professors Pound and Frankfurter were persuaded to direct a survey of criminal justice in Cleveland. Sponsored by an organization called the Cleveland Foundation, the report submitted by Pound and Frankfurter in 1922 ran to over seven hundred pages and was titled *Criminal Justice in Cleveland*.[69] As a result of his work on the Cleveland crime statistics, Frankfurter was asked to participate in a survey of crime and criminal justice in the Boston area, a project sponsored by the Harvard Corporation, the Milton Fund, and the Rockefeller Foundation. The project sought to "trace the effect of legal control on the restraint of crime and efficacy of the law's treatment of the criminal." Frankfurter contributed an introduction to the first volume of the survey's published research, *One Thousand Juvenile Delinquents*, edited by Sheldon and Eleanor Glueck, which appeared in 1934.[70]

Although a number of volumes authored by other scholars involved in the survey appeared in the 1930s, the main body of Frankfurter's own research from the project has never been published; it remains, today, a mass of typed and unorganized pages, in the possession of the Harvard Law School. The "official" history of the Law School charitably asserts that Frankfurter's failure to pursue to conclusion his work on this project was a result of his many activities on behalf of Franklin Rossevelt's New Deal.[71]

Roscoe Pound, too, was engaged in additional criminal law research as a sequel to his study of crime in Cleveland. In 1929 he was appointed by President Hoover to the Wickersham Commission, a body authorized by Congress to inquire into the enforcement of the Volstead Act's[72] prohibition of the sale of intoxicating liquors. To facilitate Pound's study of Prohibition, Harvard University gave him a leave of absence for a full academic year. The commission, largely as a result of Pound's labors, collected a huge amount of information on the enforcement of Prohibition and the criminal law in general. Even though the Commission opposed repeal of the Volstead Act, Pound's separate minority statement, in favor of abandoning this ill-advised social experiment, may have contributed to the adoption of the Twenty-First Amendment in 1933.[73]

One final instance of empirical research conducted by members of the Harvard Law School faculty was an enterprise commenced in 1924 by Frankfurter and James Landis. Landis was then a graduate student in Frankfurter's seminar on federal jurisdiction and procedure; thirteen years later he replaced Pound as the dean of the Law School. Together, the student and the professor produced a historical and quantitative study of the sweep of business of the United States Supreme Court from 1789 to the most recent October Term. This study was published in installments in the *Harvard Law Review*[74] and appeared in book form in 1928 under the title *The Business of the Supreme Court: A Study in the Federal Judicial System*.[75] It meticulously illustrated how the Supreme Court's run of business had narrowed in range but increased in quantity since the Court's eighteenth-century inception. The occasion for the publication of this study was the passage of the so-called "Judges Bill," the Judiciary Act of 1925.[76]

After Landis, a brilliant but haughty young man, received his graduate degree, he joined the Harvard law faculty. Again in collaboration with Frankfurter, he assisted in another statistical piece of legal scholarship: a survey of the sweep of the Supreme Court's business during the previous October Term. Data from this survey were published in the November 1929 issue of the *Harvard Law Review*.[77] This survey, which employed many of the same categories of analysis as were used in the 1928 volume, *The Business of the Supreme Court*, presented information on the Supreme Court's yearly business in regard to subject matter, origin, and disposition of cases, and the action of individual justices. The *Review* has continued to publish surveys of the High Court's business for all of the October Terms to the present, except for the years 1939 through 1947. Frankfurter continued to participate in these surveys until his appointment to the Supreme Court in 1939; Landis participated only until 1932, when he left for Washington to become one of the earliest academic recruits for the New Deal. Also assisting in the production of these statistical articles in the thirties were law professors Henry M. Hart, Jr., and Adrian Fisher. After 1948 the editorial staff of the *Review* compiled the data.[78] It may well be that the statistics assembled by Frankfurter and his associates for these articles on the business of the Supreme Court led to the institution in 1939 of the *Annual Report* from the director of the Administrative Office of the United States Courts. The *Annual Report*, which is still being issued, presents sundry data on the disposition of cases in all the federal courts, but its material on the U.S. Supreme Court is organized in a manner quite similar to that of the *Harvard Law Review*'s annual survey of Supreme Court business.[79]

"Cases and Materials": The Revolution in Legal Textbooks

The intellectual bickering, curricular reforms, and empirical research engaged in by the Ivy League law schools and the Johns Hopkins Institute were short-lived. By the end of the thirties, the turmoil in legal education had, for the most part, subsided. To be sure, some of the statistical research that grew out of the law school ferment was useful and important. But the curricular reforms instituted at Columbia had been thrown back by the traditionalists.

Although Yale's curricular changes were more enduring than Columbia's, they were more modest and went largely unimitated by other law schools. In 1940, just as before Oliphant and Dowling designed their functional courses in the early twenties, most law schools still employed the case method.[80] Moreover, the movement to "integrate" social science information and analysis with traditional legal study had not been successful. Teaching the social sciences in the law schools had proven too expensive and, partly because the promised benefits of a social science perspective had been overstated, the law professor's natural resistance to innovation had stiffened and finally carried the day.

Looking back at the activities at Harvard, Yale, Columbia, and Johns Hopkins in the twenties and thirties, it is possible to receive the impression that all the excitement took place at a few elite law schools and had little demonstrable, long-range impact upon legal education in general. This was not the case. All of the academic discussions in favor of new courses, on what was wrong with the case method, and on the need for more empirical research—what one legal historian has referred to as "the social sciences and all that"[81]—did lead to the development of a new type of law school casebook. The new type of casebook spread beyond the Ivy League, and, in time, found its way into most American law school classrooms. The new casebooks employed extra-legal sources and information extensively.

The casebook has, since Langdell's first book on contracts, been central to American legal education. Edwin Patterson once referred to the casebook as "the flower of American legal scholarship."[82] The first casebooks sought to fulfill a dual function: to introduce students to existing rules of law and to train students to "think like lawyers." However, the proliferation of reported court decisions in the twentieth century and the increasing skepticism about the reliability of the black-letter law, which arose within the American legal community in the interwar years, served to relegate the "primary" function (training in the "black-letter" law) to a very small niche in legal education. Partly out of an attempt to meet the "secondary function" (training the legal mind), and partly as a result of a desire in some quarters to reform the law school curriculum, casebook editors in the 1920s and 1930s began to employ novel information and materials in their published offerings. In these years, casebooks began to appear with some frequency with titles such as *Cases and Materials in Equity*, *Materials and Cases on Torts*, or simply *Materials on Contracts*. Various types of information, materials, and strategies were included in these volumes.[83] Explanatory footnotes, textnotes, and case digests commonly accompanied the printing of the usual appellate cases. Some casebooks even posed problem cases or supplemented the reported cases with probing questions. But the greatest innovations came in the so-called "revolutionary casebooks"[84] that attempted to present sundry nonlegal information and materials, mainly from the social sciences, along with appellate court opinions. Several casebooks published in the period could be termed revolutionary in their use of nonlegal information and materials. Llewellyn's *Cases and Materials on the Law of Sales*[85] is usually singled out as the first such multidisciplinary compilation. But perhaps the casebook that succeeded in most thoroughly integrating material from law and the social sciences appeared a decade later: Jerome Michael and Herbert Wechsler's *Cases and Materials on Criminal Law and its Administration: Cases, Statutes and Commentaries*.[86]

The Michael and Wechsler book was organized around central questions of legal and social policy, not around traditional categories of the criminal law. The book contained a twenty-four-page table listing the articles, books, and other publications from which selections were reprinted in the book itself. A few examples of some of the sources listed in this table indicate the variety of nonlegal information and materials included in the volume: Catherine II's instructions to the commissioners appointed to frame a new Russian code; an article from *The Nation*; newspaper accounts of trials and vigilante activities; reports of reforming and investigatory bodies, public and private; psychoanalytical literature; and excerpts from books and book reviews on criminology. These materials were not only assembled; they were "integrated"—in the best sense of the word. Overarching social policy questions provided frames for ordering the variant materials. Moreover, unlike even the best of the other "revolutionary" texts, Michael and Wechsler made substantial use of legislative documents. In a long review article on Michael and Wechsler's *Cases and Materials on Criminal Law and Its Administration*, law professor (later sociologist) David Riesman concluded:

> Their book is proof that the progressive elements in . . . jurisprudence . . . have finally overcome the period of growing pains and can pass free and adult among men. As its pattern becomes a model for the organization of equally inclusive materials around similarly vital problems of social control, we may expect a major shift in teaching, and, consequently, an improvement in the character and competence of the bar.[87]

The impact of the new or "revolutionary" casebooks on the state of legal education has been pervasive. For instance, Columbia Law School's Dean Young B. Smith noted in 1937 that thirty-six of the forty courses taught in the Law School during the previous ten years used materials prepared by the Columbia faculty. Most of these materials were drawn, in some way, from nonlegal (largely social scientific) sources. In this period, the Columbia faculty alone published 26 casebooks, 28 treatises, and 356 articles in legal and scientific journals.[88] At Yale, in 1931 alone, a dozen "new" casebooks were published.[89] Today, virtually every casebook used in courses at major American law schools contains some extra-legal materials or extra-legal information. Although most of the first generation of casebooks—Riesman preferred the term "classbook" as a more appropriate description[90]—were assembled by Ivy League law professors, many of them were adopted for classroom use at law schools all across the country. Soon professors at major mid-western and western law schools began to compile informationally oriented "classbooks" for their own use. Consequently, the most comprehensive and enduring result of the intellectual excitement in the leading American law schools in the twenties and thirties was the production of the "new" type of casebook, a still present testimony to the impact of informationally grounded thinking within the American legal community in the interwar years.

Notes

1. Even in an article as critical of the drift of American legal education in the last century as Robert Stevens's "Two Cheers for 1870: The American

Law School," 5 *Perspectives in American History* 405, 471-475 (1971), the respect for the pedagogy of Langdell is apparent. The very title of Stevens's long article is itself reflective of this measured acknowledgment of the significance of the case method in the American legal experience.

2. Josef Redlich, *The Common Law and the Case Method in American University Law Schools* (New York, 1914).

3. Quoted in William R. Johnson, *Schooled Lawyers: A Study in the Clash of Professional Cultures* (New York, 1978), p. 152.

4. Redlich, p. 35.

5. Ibid., pp. 50ff.

6. Ibid., pp. 49-50.

7. For some of the most illuminating reactions to the Redlich Report, see S.E. Baldwin, "Education for the Bar in the United States," 9 *American Political Science Review* 437 (1915); Albert Kocourek, "The Redlich Report and the Case Method," 10 *Illinois Law Review* 321 (1915); and Harlan Fiske Stone, "Dr. Redlich on the Case Method in American University Law Schools," 17 *Columbia University Quarterly* 262 (1915).

8. Alfred Z. Reed, *Training for the Public Profession of the Law* (New York, 1921).

9. Ibid., pp. 379-380.

10. Ibid., pp. 385ff.

11. Ibid., pp. 370-371.

12. The Reed Report concluded that the American legal profession at the time of World War I operated in conformance with the "facade of a unitary bar." Unlike Britain and some continental countries, America had only a single, formal class of attorneys. Yet this lack of clearly articulated class distinction did not mean that the American bar was completely democratic. In actuality, the Reed Report revealed that the important "law jobs" and most of the lucrative litigation were handled by one group of attorneys, predominantly the graduates of well-regarded law schools. Another class of attorneys, principally those who had not attended law school or were, at best, graduates of night law schools, handled the less remunerative litigation, particularly criminal cases. Reed argued that the legal profession should acknowledge the persistence of this split among lawyers and begin setting realistic and explicit requirements for admission into each "class," thus doing away with the subtle discriminatory practices then existing. Ibid., pp. 67-71, et passim. See also, on this point, Jerold Auerbach, *Unequal Justice: Lawyers and Social Change in Modern America* (New York, 1976), pp. 14-129. Reed's description of the nature of the legal profession and his suggestions for reform are almost as appropriate today as they were sixty years ago.

13. Reed, p. 346.

14. Julius Goebel, Jr., et al., *A History of the School of Law, Columbia University* (New York, 1955), p. 297; William Twining, *Karl Llewellyn and the Realist Movement* (London, 1973), p. 42. However, even before World War I, Columbia had developed a fine range of graduate offerings in the Law School. See Goebel, pp. 291-297.

15. This is the conclusion of the most careful study of the ferment in the Columbia Law School in the period, Brainerd Currie, "The Materials of Law Study, Parts I & II," 3 *Journal of Legal Education* 331,332 (1951). On the innovative law school curriculum at Columbia in the 1920s, see also Twining, pp. 41-55; Goebel, pp. 297-305; Stevens, "Two Cheers for 1870''; 471-475; and William O. Douglas, *Go East, Young Man: The Early Years* (New York, 1974), pp. 159-162.

16. Herman Oliphant, ed., *Cases on Trade Regulation* (St. Paul, 1923).

17. Quoted in Joel Seligman, *The High Citadel: The Influence of Harvard Law School* (Boston, 1978), pp. 52 and 234.

18. Douglas, p. 160.

19. Currie, "The Materials of Law Study, Parts I & II," 333-334.

20. Douglas, p. 160.

21. Herman Oliphant, ed., *Summary of Studies in Legal Education by the Faculty of Columbia University* (New York, 1928).

22. The committee members were (1) Labor: Dowling and Robert Hale; (2) Finance and Credit: Llewellyn and Moore; (3) Marketing: Oliphant and Llewellyn; (4) Business Unit: Moore, Douglas, and Carrol M. Shanks; (5) Risk and Risk Bearing: Oliphant, Young B. Smith, and Edwin Patterson; (6) Legal Administration: Smith, Roswell Magill, and Harold Medina; (7) Criminal Law: Alexander Kidd and Raymond Moley; (8) Family and Familial Property: Thomas R. Powell, Henry Moe, and John H. Johnson; (9) Legislation: Dowling, Joseph Chamberlain, and Thomas Parkinson; (10) Historical and Comparative Jurisprudence: Yntema and Goebel. See Oliphant, *Summary of Studies in Legal Education by the Faculty of Columbia University*, pp. 22-23.

23. Quoted in Seligman, pp. 52 and 234.

24. See generally Brainerd Currie, "The Materials of Law Study, Part III," 8 *Journal of Legal Education* 1, 64-76 (1955). William Twining has provided a useful delineation of the two factions in his *Karl Llewellyn and the Realist Movement*, pp. 54-67. Those who defended the functional courses and the need for empirical research to make the courses viable he calls the Scientists: Oliphant, Moore, Douglas, Yntema, and Marshall. Those who may have sympathized with the former group's contextual approach but resisted its apparent wish to turn Columbia Law School into

a community of scholars, spending most of their time engaged in empirical research, he dubs the Prudents (from the Latin phrase *prudentia juris*, that is, those concerned more with the craft of the law than its scholarly study). This latter group included Dowling, Goebel, Harold Medina, Jerome Michael, Edwin Patterson, Young B. Smith, and Karl Llewellyn.

25. Stevens, "Two Cheers for 1870," 475-476.

26. Robert M. Hutchins, "The Autobiography of an Ex-Law Student," 1 *University of Chicago Law Review* 511, 512-513 (1934).

27. Ibid., 513.

28. Quoted in Seligman, p. 63.

29. Douglas, pp. 160-161.

30. Walter Wheeler Cook, "Scientific Method and the Law," 13 *American Bar Association Journal* 303, 309 (1927). On the Johns Hopkins Institute, see also Twining, pp. 60-67; Wilfrid E. Rumble, Jr., *American Legal Realism: Skepticism, Reform, and the Judicial Process* (Ithaca, N.Y., 1968), pp. 15-20; and Rumble, "The Foundations of American Legal Realism" (Unpublished Ph.D. Dissertation: Johns Hopkins University, 1962), passim.

31. Rumble, *American Legal Realism*, pp. 15-16; and James Willard Hurst, *The Growth of American Law: The Law Makers* (Boston, 1950), p. 170.

32. Leon C. Marshall, "The Institute of Law, Johns Hopkins University," 2 *American Scholar* 115, 115 (1933).

33. (Baltimore, 1933).

34. Ibid., pp. 1-2.

35. Marshall, "The Institute of Law," 115.

36. For bibliographies of the studies produced by scholars at the Institute of Law, see Rumble, "The Foundations of American Legal Realism," p. 73, note 105; and Twining, pp. 403-404, note 20.

37. Frederick K. Beutel, quoted in Rumble, *American Legal Realism*, p. 19.

38. On the Yale Law School in the twenties and thirties and on the early years of the Institute for Human Relations, see Twining, pp. 62-69; Douglas, pp. 163-175; Stevens, "Two Cheers for 1870," 478-480; Thurman Arnold, *Fair Fights and Foul* (New York, 1955), pp. 57-68; and Dorothy S. Thomas, "Some Aspects of Socio-Legal Research at Yale," 37 *American Journal of Sociology* 213 (1931); and Charles E. Clark, "The Education and Scientific Objectives of the Yale Law School," 167 *Annals of the American Academy of Political and Social Sciences* 165 (1933).

39. On the work of Clark and his associates, see Charles E. Clark and Harry Shulman, *A Study of Law Administration in Connecticut: A Report of an Investigation of the Activities of Certain Trial Courts of the State*

(New Haven, 1937); and Clark and Shulman, "Jury Trials in Civil Cases—A Study in Judicial Administration," 43 *Yale Law Journal* 867 (1934). On the work of Douglas and his associates, see William Clark, William O. Douglas, and Dorothy Thomas, "Business Failures Project—A Problem in Methodology," 39 *Yale Law Journal* 1013 (1930); Douglas and Thomas, "Business Failures Project—II: An Analysis of Methods of Investigation," 40 *Yale Law Journal* 1034 (1931); Douglas, "Some Functional Aspects of Bankruptcy," 41 *Yale Law Journal* 329 (1932); Douglas, "Wage Earner Bankruptcies—State vs. Federal Control," 42 *Yale Law Journal* 591 (1933); Josef H. Furth, "Critical Period Before Bankruptcy," 41 *Yale Law Journal* 853 (1932); Emma Corstvet, "Inadequate Bookkeeping as a Factor in Business Failure," 45 *Yale Law Journal* 1201 (1936); and Douglas and J. Howard Marshall, "A Factual Study of Bankruptcy Administration and Some Suggestions," 32 *Columbia Law Review* 25 (1932). On the work of Moore and his collaborators, see Underhill Moore and Gilbert Sussman, "Legal and Institutional Methods Applied to the Debiting of Direct Discounts," 40 *Yale Law Journal* 381, 555, 752, 928, 1055, 1219 (1931); Moore and Theodore S. Hope, Jr., "An Institutional Approach to the Law of Commercial Banking," 38 *Yale Law Journal* 703 (1929); C.E. Brand, Moore, and Sussman, "Legal and Institutional Methods Applied to Orders to Stop Payment of Checks," 42 *Yale Law Journal* 817, 1198 (1933); Moore, Sussman, and Corstvet, "Drawing Against Uncollected Checks," 45 *Yale Law Journal* 1, 260 (1935); Charles C. Callahan and Moore, "Law and Learning Theory: A Study in Legal Control," 53 *Yale Law Journal* 1 (1943); Clark L. Hull, "Moore and Callahan's 'Law and Learning Theory': A Psychologist's Impressions," 53 *Yale Law Journal* 330 (1944); Hessel E. Yntema, " 'Law and Learning Theory' Through the Looking Glass of Legal History," 53 *Yale Law Journal* 338 (1944); and F.S.C. Northrop, "Underhill Moore's Legal Science: Its Nature and Significance," 59 *Yale Law Journal* 196 (1950). Other statistically oriented articles appearing in the *Yale Law Journal* in the late 1920s and the 1930s include John R. Commons and E.W. Morehouse, "Legal and Economic Job Analysis," 37 *Yale Law Journal* 139 (1927); Don E. Cooper and Wesley Sturges, "Credit Administration and Wage Earner Bankruptcies," 42 *Yale Law Journal* 487 (1933); Walter Gellhorn, "Federal Workmen's Compensation for Transportation Employees," 43 *Yale Law Journal* 906 (1934); and Philip M. Glick, "Federal Subsistence Homesteads Program," 44 *Yale Law Journal* 1324 (1935).

40. Clark and Shulman, "Jury Trials in Civil Cases," 43 *Yale Law Journal* 867, 869-874 (1934); James Willard Hurst, *The Growth of American Law*, pp. 172-174.

41. Clark and Shulman, "Jury Trials in Civil Cases," 880-884.

42. William Clark, Douglas, and Thomas, "Business Failures Project—A Problem in Methodology," 39 *Yale Law Journal* 1013 (1930); and Douglas and Thomas, "Business Failures Project—II: An Analysis of Methods of Investigation," 40 *Yale Law Journal* 1034 (1931).

43.Douglas and J. Howard Marshall, "A Factual Study of Bankruptcy Administration and Some Suggestions," 32 *Columbia Law Review* 25 (1932); and Douglas, "Wage Earner Bankruptcies," 42 *Yale Law Journal* 591 (1933).

44. Certainly Douglas, himself, believed this was the case. See Douglas, *Go East, Young Man*, p. 175.

45. See F.S.C. Northrop, "Underhill Moore's Legal Science: Its Nature and Significance," 59 *Yale Law Journal* 196 (1950).

46. For concise explanations of the "institutional method," see Northrop, "Underhill Moore's Legal Science;" and Rumble, *American Legal Realism*, pp. 161-166.

47. Northrop, "Underhill Moore's Legal Science," 197; and Twining, pp. 63-66.

48. Moore and Sussman, "Legal and Institutional Methods Applied to the Debiting of Direct Discounts," 40 *Yale Law Journal* 381, 555, 752, 928, 1055, 1219 (1931). The theoretical foundation for Moore's empirical institutional studies of banking is found in Moore and Hope, "An Institutional Approach to the Law of Commercial Banking," 38 *Yale Law Journal* 703 (1929).

49. *Callahan* v. *Bank of Anderson*, 69 S.C. 374, 48 S.E. 293 (1904) (lower court decision allowed to stand as upper court evenly divided).

50. *Delano* v. *Equitable Trust Co.*, 110 Misc. 704, 181 N.Y. Supp. 852 (Sup. Ct. 1920); *Goldstein* v. *Jefferson Title & Trust Co.*, 95 Pa. Super. Ct. 167 (1928).

51. Moore and Sussman, "Legal and Institutional Methods Applied to the Debiting of Direct Discounts," 559.

52. Ibid., 752, 928, 1055.

53. Ibid., 1249-1250.

54. See Brand, Moore, and Sussman, "Legal and Institutional Methods Applied to Orders to Stop Payment of Checks," 42 *Yale Law Journal* 817, 1198 (1933); Moore, Sussman, and Corstvet, "Drawing Against Uncollected Checks," 45 *Yale Law Journal* 1,260 (1935).

55. 53 *Yale Law Journal* 1 (1943).

56. Rumble, *American Legal Realism*, p. 162, note 45. Yet it should be noted that Llewellyn was not particularly enamored of this "philosophy." In 1956 he referred to Moore's Parking and traffic studies as the "nadir of idiocy." Quoted in Twining, p. 63.

57. Charles E. Clark, "Underhill Moore," 59 *Yale Law Journal* 189, 191 (1950).

58. Northrop, "Underhill Moore's Legal Science, 196." Similarly, political scientist Glendon Schubert has remarked that "it was Moore's fortune to be at least a quarter century ahead of his time, and to be writing for the wrong profession to boot." Glendon Schubert, ed., *Judicial Behavior: A Reader in Theory and Research* (Chicago, 1964), p. 13.

59. Stevens, "Two Cheers for 1870," 477-478, note. 43.

60. According to Douglas: "The whole Yale Law project gradually faded. The total effect of the Institute and of all our efforts was zero, because we could not find enough people who were willing to devote effort to such matters." Douglas, *Go East, Young Man*, p. 170.

61. Quoted in Charles Warren, *History of the Harvard Law School and of Early Legal Conditions in America* (New York, 1908), II, p. 374.

62. See William O. Douglas, "Education for the Law," in James Allen, ed., *Democracy and Finance: The Addresses and Public Statements of William O. Douglas as a Member and Chairman of the Securities and Exchange Commission* (New Haven, 1940), pp. 285-286. See also Douglas, *Go East, Young Man*, pp. 160, 169-170.

63. David Wigdor, *Roscoe Pound: Philosopher of Law* (Westport, Conn., 1974), p. 224; and Seligman, p. 63.

64. W. Barton Leach, quoted in Wigdor, p. 249.

65. On Pound's deanship, see Wigdor, pp. 203-254; and Arthur E. Sutherland, *The Law at Harvard: A History of Ideas and Men, 1817-1967* (Cambridge, Mass., 1967), pp. 243-299; and Seligman, pp. 47-67.

66. Sutherland, p. 287.

67. Seligman, p. 61.

68. Arnold, p. 58.

69. (Cleveland, 1922).

70. (Boston, 1934).

71. See Sutherland, p. 273.

72. 41 Stat. 305 (1919).

73. Sutherland, pp. 274-275. On the statistical research of Pound and Frankfurter, see also Wigdor, pp. 245-248.

74. "The Business of the Supreme Court," 38 *Harvard Law Review* 1005 (1925); 39 *Harvard Law Review* 35 (1925); 39 *Harvard Law Review* 325, 587, 1046 (1926); 40 *Harvard Law Review* 431, 834, 1110 (1927).

75. Felix Frankfurter and James M. Landis, *The Business of the Supreme Court: A Study in the Federal Judicial System* (New York, 1928).

76. 43 Stat. 936 (1925). By rewriting the jurisdictional rules of the federal system, this Act relieved the Supreme Court of the obligation of hearing many "unimportant" cases and, at the same time, granted the justices

greater freedom and time to devote their attention to what they considered to be the important cases. This act made the discretionary *certiorari* jurisdiction the main procedural route to the Supreme Court docket. Thus, the Judiciary Act allowed the justices to consider for hearing thousands of cases, but gave these men virtually complete authority over which of those cases would be given full hearings. After the passage of the Judges Bill, the Supreme Court became, in terms of the control of its own docket, a "high court," similar to the Court of Appeals in England. On the significance of the Judiciary Act of 1925, see Frankfurter and Landis, *The Business of the Supreme Court*, pp. 299-318, et passim; Richard J. Richardson and Kenneth N. Vines, *The Politics of Federal Courts: Lower Courts in the United States* (Boston, 1970), pp. 142-161; John W. Johnson, "The Dimensions of Non-Legal Evidence in the American Judicial Process: The United States Supreme Court's Use of Extra-Legal Materials in the Twentieth Century" (Unpublished Ph.D. Dissertation: University of Minnesota, 1974), pp. 168-177; William Howard Taft, "Jurisdiction of the Supreme Court Under the Act of February 13, 1925," 35 *Yale Law Journal* 1 (1925); and Merlo J. Pusey, "The 'Judges Bill' After Half a Century," *Yearbook 1976: Supreme Court Historical Society* 73 (1976).

77. Felix Frankfurter and James Landis, "The Business of the Supreme Court at October Term, 1928," 43 *Harvard Law Review* 33 (1929).

78. Normally, the November issue of the *Harvard Law Review* contains a discussion of the important matters considered by the Supreme Court in the previous October Term. Most of these issues also display the statistics on the Court's run of business in the Term just completed. Occasionally, though, the *Review* has chosen to present data for two or more Terms in a single issue.

79. (Washington, D.C.). See Johnson, "The Dimensions of Non-Legal Evidence in the American Judicial Process," 316-317, note 40.

80. See Stevens, "Two Cheers for 1870," 481-482; Douglas, *Go East, Young Man*, p. 170.

81. Stevens, "Two Cheers for 1870," 470.

82. "Book Review: Chafee and Simpson, *Cases on Equity Jurisdiction and Specific Performance* (1934)," 48 *Harvard Law Review* 1261, 1261 (1935).

83. On the development of new casebooks in the twenties and thirties, see Albert Ehrenzweig, "The American Casebook: 'Cases and Materials,' " 32 *Georgetown Law Journal* 224 (1944).

84. This term was first used by Ehrenzweig. Ibid., 231-241.

85. (Chicago, 1930).

86. (Chicago, 1940). Other casebooks published in the period deserve mention for their use of substantial extra-legal information and materials,

for example, Walter Gellhorn, *Cases and Comments on Administrative Law* (Chicago, 1940); Philip W. Thayer, *Cases and Materials in the Law Merchant* (Cambridge, Mass., 1939); and Roscoe Steffen, *Cases on Commercial and Investment Paper* (Chicago, 1939).

87. David Riesman, "Law and Social Science: A Report on Michael and Wechsler's Classbook on Criminal Law and Administration," 50 *Yale Law Journal* 636, 653 (1940).

88. See Goebel, p. 331.

89. See Stevens, "Two Cheers for 1870," 483-484.

90. Riesman, "Law and Social Science," passim.

7
INFORMATION AND THE CRUCIBLE OF LEGAL REALISM

This study until now has conspicuously ignored the role of legal philosophy in relation to the penchant for information. The reason for this is simple, although no doubt debatable. The early twentieth-century partisans of Brandeis briefs, those associated with the new extra-legal sources of information, the champions of legislative history, and those who undertook empirical social science research into legal subjects may have been intellectually sympathetic to certain strains of legal philosophy, but their commitment to information grew out of the more specific concerns already discussed, not out of devotion to a certain school of legal thought. Hence, most of the discussions of legal philosophy in the early twentieth century were explanatory and rationalizing rather than causative. In other words, legal philosophy in the first three decades of the twentieth century was not at the heart of American legal culture. It was reflective rather than generative. It was related to the informational mind-set only to the degree that the shadows in Plato's famous cave metaphor were related to the objects they represented in the fire light.

American legal philosophy, however, came out into the sunlight in 1930. A famous exchange of views between Roscoe Pound and Karl Llewellyn beginning in that year set the most influential voices in the country's legal community talking about something called "legal realism."[1] Since 1930 it has been almost impossible to conceive of discourse about American legal thought or behavior that did not take note of the realist movement. Legal realism, hard as it was to define and isolate, seemed to assume a life of its own in the thirties, with so-called realistice thought becoming the principal component of the informational paradigm. With the advent of the realist movement, American legal philosophy had moved out of its cave and into the glare of the legal community's scrutiny. Also, with the accession of the realist mood in American jurisprudence, the penchant for information had reached its greatest intensity among the elite members of the country's legal profession.

A great deal of ink has been expended in the last half century or so in an attempt to define legal realism.[2] "Legal Realism" is a term like Romanticism or Classicism; it has plenty of connotations but no single denotation. A fair, working understanding of the term would hold that legal realism represented a general outlook rather than a single school of thought, a loose amalgam of heterodox ideas held by a number of articulate and prolific legal scholars, lawyers, and judges. It blossomed in the twenties and grew to full flower in the thirties. What tied the realists together in the eyes of the larger legal community was both their skepticism regarding traditional legal maxims and institutions and their endorsement of empirical research to determine how legal systems in fact operated.

To grasp the significance of realism, it is necessary first to retreat into the cave to examine its shadowy antecedents. For as English scholar William Twining has maintained, "the realist movement must be treated historically before it can be satisfactorily dealt with analytically."[3] The following discussion of early twentieth-century American legal philosophy is not meant to be comprehensive. Rather, its purpose is simply to illuminate the informational dimension of such thinking in the period and to reveal its links to the realist movement.

Holmes, Sociological Jurisprudence, and the Antecedents to Realism

The place of Oliver Wendell Holmes in American legal history is large but by no means clearly understood.[4] Holmes's reputation as a legal philosopher stems from one long work, *The Common Law*, published in 1881,[5] and a series of occasional speeches, essays, and letters drafted at various points during his long career as a judge.[6] His writings, with the exception of *The Common Law*, were not works that benefited from quiet reflection. Holmes never took the opportunity to write a comprehensive book pulling together his various views on the law. His reputation as a philosopher flows from a few remarkable epigrammatic statements that other later thinkers have found particularly inspiring. In referring to the influence on the legal realists of the man whom Justice Benjamin Cardozo once called "the great overlord of the law and its philosophy,"[7] Karl Llewellyn claimed that from Holmes "we all derive."[8]

There appear to be two Holmesian statements that especially called forth the praise of the realists. The first is at the beginning of *The Common Law*:

The life of the law has not been logic: it has been experience. The felt necessities of the time, the prevalent moral and political theories, intuitions of public policy, avowed or unconscious, even the prejudices which judges share with their fellow-men, have had a good deal more to do than the syllogism in determining the rules by which men should be governed.[9]

The other is contained in his 1897 address, "The Path of the Law," delivered at the dedication of a new hall for the Boston University School of Law:

Take the fundamental question, What constitutes the law? . . . The prophecies of what the courts will do in fact, and nothing more pretentious, are what I mean by the law.[10]

Juxtaposed as they are here, these two statements appear contradictory. This is not unusual when considering selected quotations from Holmes's writings out of context. In Holmes, something could (and can) be found for legal thinkers of almost every persuasion.[11]

In the statement from *the Common Law*, Holmes appears to be saying that court decisions and legislative enactments can be understood only by examining their place in the ebb and flow of life. It follows from this that extra-legal insights and information may frequently help one grasp legal rules. In the second statement,

Holmes seems to ignore the extra-legal factors that might bear upon an understanding of the law, and he submits that legal thinking involves only the art of predicting what actions courts will take. Of course, in the second statement much is left for implication. In any case, from statements such as these, it was claimed by later writers that Holmes saw the difficulty of ever achieving certainty in the legal sphere, that he supported the inquiry into extra-legal factors that might have influenced judicial decisions, that he endorsed the need to marshall extra-legal information to aid court decision making, that he advocated the need to investigate what courts in fact do and not what they say, and that he believed firmly in the importance of keeping the law separate from moral considerations.[12]

In line with some of these characterizations of Holmes's philosophy is the well-regarded view of intellectual historian Morton White.[13] According to White, Holmes's thought—as characteristically expressed in the above quoted passages—can be understood as one component of a "revolt against formalism." In White's judgment, the years between 1890 and 1920 saw a few leading American intellectuals in diverse fields such as philosophy, economics, history, and law becoming suspicious of the excessively formal approaches of their respective disciplines: John Dewey and William James reacted against Hegelian dialectics and founded a philosophical school with a decidedly practical orientation (that is, "pragmatism"); Thorstein Veblen rejected the patterned dicta of classical economics; Charles Beard and James Harvey Robinson sought to uncover the economic motives of historical figures and began to write their own history in a purposive fashion; finally, Holmes was led to castigate those theories of jurisprudence that were based upon moral or natural law postulates and did not take into account the discrete actions of individual judges.[14] For White, Holmes was the father of legal realism.[15]

It is doubtful that Holmes himself would have taken credit for spawning legal realism. Holmes resisted identifying himself as part of any group. Although some of his opinions and off-the-bench writings contained the seeds of skepticism and empiricism, others were decidedly antirealist. For example, in a letter to his longtime friend Harold Laski, Holmes admitted that he hated facts. In commenting upon a discussion that he and his good friend and colleague

Louis Brandeis had had regarding the need for sustained factual study, Holmes admitted that it might be good for him "to get into actualities," but that he "would rather meditate on the initial push and the following spin."[16] Similarly, Holmes's opinion in *American Banana Company* v. *United Fruit Company*[17] shows a decidedly antirealist, conceptual bias. In that case, Holmes wrote a majority opinion that ignored several material facts. In denying the suit of a small corporation against a giant, international conglomerate, Holmes refused to take into account the actual behavior of the United Fruit Company, which had used its influence to get the Costa Rican army to seize the plaintiff's small plantation. In a typically terse opinion, Holmes concluded that the plaintiff company had no basis for its suit since an American court could not contest the "pure fact" of Costa Rican sovereignty. For legal purposes, it had to be assumed, Holmes said, that the Costa Rican army was acting with the consent of the government.[18] the "pure facts," of course, flew in the face of the real, factual situation.[19]

In spite of these indications that Holmes was not committed to serious empirical scrutiny, many of the later realists claimed him as their intellectual father. Jerome Frank, one of the most vocal and interesting representatives of realist thought, called Holmes the first "non-Euclidian," "completely adult jurist."[20] Frank must have had Holmes's aphorisms from *The Common Law* and "The Path of the Law" more in mind than his holding in *American Banana Company* v. *United Fruit Company.*

If Holmes was a questionable parent for realism, Roscoe Pound—the distinguished legal philosopher, Harvard Law School dean, and trained botanist—was a more likely source of the movement's paternity. The irony here is that Pound, like Holmes, resisted affiliation with the realists. In fact, in the thirties Pound became one of the movement's staunchest opponents.[21] If Holmes had a gift for composing aphorisms that inspired later scholars, Pound had a similarly unique ability to coin brief phrases to which later realists often seemed to genuflect. The titles of some of his most famous articles—"Mechanical Jurisprudence,"[22] "Law in Books and Law in Action,"[23] and "The Need of a Sociological Jurisprudence,"[24]—contained some of the most famous of his catchphrases. Pound may not have been the first American jurisprudent to focus on the need to examine the social origins and effects of legal rules, but his advocacy of this necessary research orientation was more strident than that of any other early twentieth-century legal writer. Pound had left the Harvard Law School without a degree in 1890; twenty years later he returned to Harvard as the Story Professor of Law. In the interim, Pound had studied for and received the Ph.D. in Botany from the University of Nebraska, had practiced law, had served as a commissioner to the Nebraska Supreme Court, had taught in the University of Nebraska and University of Chicago law schools, had served as dean of the Nebraska Law School, and had started a remarkable career of legal scholarship.

"Sociological jurisprudence," the forerunner of legal realism, became identified with Pound more than with any other legal thinker of the period.[25] As Pound conceived of it, sociological jurisprudence involved a break from the "method of deduction from predetermined conceptions"; it was a "movement for pragmatism as a philosophy of law."[26] Pound's version of sociological jurisprudence also emphasized the importance of procuring factual data about the law in action and stressed cooperation with the social sciences in order to obtain insights into legal behavior.[27] Like Holmes, Pound believed that scholars should seek a knowlege of the operation of law in all of the complexities of its social setting. But contrary to Holmes, Pound's sociological jurisprudence contained little skepticism and almost no moral relativism.[28] These departures from Holmes's legal philosophy ultimately led Pound to renounce the younger realists of the twenties and thirties.

Although Pound was an eloquent spokesman for the need for fact-centered legal scholarship, his own writings promised more than they delivered. Although Pound was one of the first law professors to engage in a large-scale empirical research project—the Cleveland crime survey of the early twenties—Pound's allegiance was more to the common law tradition than to the new social sciences.[29] In the twenties, Pound was one of the principal movers behind the formation of the conceptually oriented American Law Institute. In 1924, at the behest of the Institute, Pound published an essay on the "Classification of the Law"[30] that took no account whatsoever of the social contexts of the legal principles he classified. A scholar, commenting on this essay of Pound's, observed that it "might well have been written by someone who had never heard of 'sociological jurisprudence.' "[31]

Perhaps the direction of Pound's scholarship after 1920 was blunted and then stifled by his administrative responsibilities as Harvard's Law School dean and his service on various commissions and investigatory bodies. Whatever the reason, most of Pound's scholarly activity after World War I was aimed more at celebrating the Anglo-American common law tradition than at assembling data on the law in action.[32] In 1936, as one of his last official acts as dean of the Law School, Pound was asked to organize a Law School conference in celebration of the tricentennial of the founding of Harvard University. For his own address for this event, delivered in the midst of the country's grave constitutional crisis over New Deal legislation, Pound chose the rather prosaic topic, "The Future of the Common Law."[33]

Besides Holmes and Pound, the realists were influenced by other legal thinkers of the pre-World War I period. John Chipman Gray of Harvard and Arthur Corbin and Wesley Hohfeld of Yale are sometimes regarded as having written essays on the philosophy of law from which the realists drew sustenance.[34] However, their writings spoke principally of the skeptical, moral relativism that some of the realists were later to espouse. None of these men was a leading advocate of empiricism.

Without question, the leading advocate of legal empiricism in this country before the raising of voices by the realists was Louis Brandeis. As has been noted, Brandeis led by example as well as by his rhetoric. He did not write cogent, well-reasoned articles in defense of the place of statistics and other data in the judicial process. Instead, he offered the data himself in his briefs and opinions. Frequently, Brandeis's compilations of data were followed by pleas for greater use of such information. The apologies for empiricism in his legal writings were not, of course, as carefully framed or as fully developed as they would have been if written for a law journal. Yet, that should not disqualify them as important contributions to legal philosophy. Brandeis has generally been credited with putting sociological jurisprudence into practice,[35] but he should also be regarded as a legal philosopher and an important influence on the realists.

Sociological Jurisprudence, Progressivism, and the Impact of World War I

Since Brandeis, Pound, Holmes, and the other advocates of sociological jurisprudence claimed that the law operated within a social context, it is logical that their own ideas about the law were influenced by the swirl of events and the climate of opinion in the early twentieth century. In a rough sense, the ideas of these men were related to certain strains of the Progressive Movement in the period 1900-17.[36] "Progressivism," inside and outside of government, was dominated by the belief that society was constantly in flux and not governed by ineluctable, social Darwinistic rules. The Progressives maintained that American life could be improved by proper governmental management and regulation. In order to grasp the real impact of industrialization, urbanization, and immigration on American life, the Progressives endorsed empirical studies of social phenomena. They were convinced that the data from these inquiries would be useful in understanding the dimensions of the country's problems and would, accordingly, provide a basis for suggesting appropriate legislative remedies.[37]

The field of social welfare, which came alive in the Progressive era, seemed particularly consumed by facts. Beginning with a spate of confessional literature published in the late 1890s, the early "muckrakers" labored to reveal the accurate and depressing conditions in the country's cities. Around the turn of the century, a group of social welfare workers, including Jane Addams and Jacob Riis, founded a magazine titled *Charities*, which had as its purpose "the undertaking of important pieces of social investigation not provided for by any existing organizations."[38] The magazine was later retitled *The Survey* and became known for sponsoring a number of detailed empirical inquiries into labor and living conditions in urban areas. Under the able direction of Paul Kellogg, *The Survey* became a major force in bringing information on social ills to the attention of policymakers.[39] Just as the legal community was preoccupied by a penchant for information in the early twentieth century, so too was the field of social welfare and, by implication, the Progressive Movement generally.

Besides being committed to empirical research as a necessary prelude to social change, most of the Progressives were fervent optimists. They believed that efficient social engineering could bring about a better world. Their optimism was founded upon a firm moral basis. The Progressives were not afraid to distinguish good from bad, even to the degree of foisting their own moral standards on society as a whole. It was no accident that the Progressive Movement coincided with Prohibition and a vigorous campaign against prostitution.[40]

The moralism of the Progressives was mirrored in the pre-World War I views of some of the sociological jurisprudents, notably Brandeis and Pound. The Brandeis briefs and the Brandeis opinions were premised on their author's firm conviction that he (together with Josephine Goldmark, Felix Frankfurter, and fellow researchers) knew what was best for those individuals "protected" by minimum-wage and maximum-hours laws. Pound had a similar view of the essential moral core of law. In an article published in 1912, "The Scope and Purpose of Sociological Jurisprudence,"[41] Pound asserted that adherents to the new school of legal thinking:

conceive of the legal rule as a general guide to the judge, leading him to the just result, but insist that within wide limits he should be free to deal with the individual case, so as to meet the demands of justice between the parties and accord with the general reason of ordinary men.[42]

Only Holmes, of the sociological jurisprudents writing before World War I, refused to claim that law was founded or should be founded upon a moral basis. He preferred to conceive of the law as did his archetypal "bad man," introduced in "The Path of the Law" address. The bad man, Holmes said, cared little about the basis for the law; he did, however, care very much about what the courts did and what the courts might do should he act in certain ways.[43] Holmes's moral relativism—some would call it cynicism—was prescient.

World War I profoundly altered the content and tone of intellectual thought in this country as well as in Europe.[44] The war did not kill the Progressive Movement,[45] but it did cause the majority of progressive thinkers to lose much of their optimism and come away from the war experience with grave doubts about whether man any longer resided in a moral universe. Legal philosophy was similarly affected. Although Pound continued to speak of legal morality with conviction but less and less originality,[46] the most characteristic statements of legal writers of the first few years after the war were coated with skepticism. For example, writing in 1922, Charles Grove Haines, a political scientist, suggested that judges' decisions were not necessarily founded upon precedent or a sense of justice but upon a whole catalog of personal, psychological, political, and economic influences.[47] For Haines and a number of other scholars of the early twenties,[48] the law was no longer founded upon moral or legal certainty—if, in fact, it ever had been.

Even judges themselves, in their off-the-bench commentary, admitted to uncertainty and skepticism in their own decision making. The scholarly Benjamin Cardozo, then a New York Court of Appeals judge, confessed in his 1921 Storrs Lectures at Yale University that the taught tradition of the law occasionally had to give way in the mind of judges to forces "deep below consciousness . . . , the likes and dislikes, the predilections and the prejudices, the complex of instincts and emotions and habits and convictions, which make the . . . judge."[49] A Few years later, another sitting jurist—Federal District Judge Joseph Hutcheson—admitted to similar uncertainty in an article whose very title, "The Judgment Intuitive: The Function of the 'Hunch' in Judicial Decision,"[50] must have scandalized a moralist like Pound.

The Birth of Legal Realism

For several reasons, it is difficult to demarcate the realist movement from other strains of legal thought in America. First, it was never widely recognized as a "movement—even by its adherents—until after its original center had fragmented. Second, the realists published no specialized journal, held no annual meetings, and granted no awards. Finally, many of those labeled as realists were highly critical of each other—both intellectually and personally. As a result, a good case could be made that no realist "Movement" ever existed. However, in retrospect, it is clear that a largely unconscious bonding was evident among certain law professors in the late 1920s that was unlike any other intellectual affiliation in American legal history.

If the realist movement had a beginning at a definite time and place, it was in the mid-1920s at the Columbia Law School when Columbia's law faculty committed itself to a serious study of the law school curriculum along functional lines. The Columbia reformers did not call themselves realists or even legal philosophers. They were principally concerned with designing courses reflective of the way law operated in the real world; they were not legal philosophers except in the most pragmatic sense. Nevertheless, what Professors Oliphant, Moore, Yntema, Douglas, and the other leading functionalists at Columbia proposed had profound philosophical implications. By encouraging the detailed examination of the way the law operated in the social context instead of promoting a study of what the appellate courts said was the law or what scholars said the law should be, the realists were charged with being moral relativists and crude empiricists. In suggesting that the law was influenced by various extra-legal forces, that it was by no means fixed or certain, the Columbia reformers were branded as pseudoscientists and traitors to the common law tradition. It was in response to criticisms such as these that the Columbia functionalists drew together and began to appear, at least in the eyes of the legal community as a whole, to endorse a peculiar and controversial set of ideas.

At Columbia in the late twenties were four of the most empirically minded of the soon-to-be realists: Underhill Moore, William O. Douglas, Herman Oliphant, and Hessel Yntema. Also at Columbia in 1928 was Karl Llewellyn, perhaps the most influential of the realists. Other members of the Columbia faculty at the time, who would later be labeled as realists, included Edwin Patterson, Noel Dowling, Julius Goebel, Jerome Michael, Samuel Klaus, and L.A. Tulin.[51] Most of these men were involved in the campaign for a functional curiculum; many of them were later to edit casebooks that would draw upon social science data and other extra-legal information; a few would themselves undertake important empirical studies; and one, Llewellyn, would become the intellectual bellwether for the realist movement. When the schism over the functional curriculum occurred in 1928, some of the Columbia functionalists went elsewhere in search of academic climates hospitable to legal skepticism and empirical research. Douglas and Moore accepted appointments under Dean Hutchins at the Yale Law School, and Olipant and Yntema took advantage of the opportunity to participate in the newly established Johns Hopkins Institute of Law.

The splintering of the Columbia faculty was unfortunate because it broke apart an uncommonly innovative faculty, but it did not spell the end of realism.[52] Under the abbreviated deanship of Robert Hutchins, the Yale Law School was able to attract and nurture another "Bloomsburyesque Group" of realists.[53] Besides Douglas, Moore, and Hutchins himself, the Yale cadres included Thurman Arnold, Wesley Sturges, Charles Clark, E.G. Lorenzen, Fred Rodell, and (in his early years) Myres McDougal. Although the most important realist critique of the traditional law school curriculum had taken place at Columbia in the late twenties, the Yale Law School in the thirties was the center of empirical legal research, highlighted by the curious but seminal studies of Underhill Moore. Besides promoting empirical legal research, the realist faction in the Yale Law School took delight in criticizing the conceptual, highly formalistic Restatement. Moreover, the Yale professors were at least as persistent as their Columbia counterparts in promoting interdisciplinary exchanges. In the twenties, the Columbia law professors had sought intellectual sustenance from business administration and anthropology; in the thirties, the Yale professors looked primarily to psychology and economics.

In the important year of 1930, American legal philosophy took a critical (some would say "unfortunate") step in explicitly recognizing the existence of a new mode in American legal thought. Only in 1930—after the birth, brief life, and abrupt death of the functional curriculum at Columbia; and after the efforts of the Yale Law School and the Johns Hopkins Institute to recruit legal scientists—did the term legal realism become part of the lingua franca of the American legal community. If a legal realist "movement" did exist, it subsumed the activities of the functional reformers at Columbia and the early years of research by the legal scientists at Johns Hopkins and Yale. Hence, the initial thrust and perhaps even the most crucial phase of legal realism occurred before the legal community was able to devise a proper appellation for the "movement."

   The term legal realism may have been used in the twenties, but
it was given its first widespread exposure in American legal circles
with the publication of three law review articles in 1930 and 1931.
The first article, "A Realistic Jurisprudence—The Next Step,"
appeared in the *Columbia Law Review*.[54] Its author was the relatively young Columbia law professor Karl Llewellyn. Llewellyn
had, in a limited way, supported the curricular reforms at Columbia
in the twenties, but he had refused to resign when the functional
program was scuttled. His essay, after a rambling argument, came
to the conclusion that the most "fruitful" recent thinking about
the law "involved moves toward ever-decreasing emphasis on
words, and ever-increasing emphasis on observable behavior."[55]
Without specifying to any great degree which legal thinkers he saw
as "realists," Llewellyn singled out Roscoe Pound, the Harvard
Law School dean and perhaps the foremost of the sociological
jurisprudents, for a mixture of praise and criticism. He claimed
that although Pound had long campaigned for the study of the law
in a social context, he had not concretized sociological jurisprudence.
That is, Pound's research, Llewellyn believed, had not really pene-
trated to a disclosure of the "law in action."[56]

   In March 1931, Dean Pound took the opportunity to respond to
Llewellyn's article in the pages of the *Harvard Law Review*.[57]
Pound's article was a short, hastily composed piece[58] that was
highly critical of what its author described as "the call for a realistic jurisprudence . . . on the part of our younger teachers of law."[59]
Uncharacteristically for Pound, the article contained no footnotes
and named no names in its blanket indictment of the so-called
realism. Among other things, Pound charged that these "younger
teachers" had a "faith in masses of figures as having significance
in and of themselves,"[60] that they were too concerned with psychology and not enough concerned with history or ethics,[61] and that
they tended to "deny that there are rules or principles or conceptions or doctrines at all."[62]

   It is unlikely that Llewellyn's *Columbia Law Review* article, by
itself, provoked such a strong response from Pound. In actuality,
Pound's antipathy to the views of the "younger teachers" had
been festering for years and just took this occasion to burst into

print. As previously noted, Pound was not at all sympathetic to the curricular reforms championed by these teachers at Yale and Columbia. Although Pound's sociological jurisprudence was the acknowledged starting point for the ideas of many of the realists,[63] he found several reasons—not all of them intellectual—to attack his disciples. He was offended by the bluntness of the realists, disturbed by what he wrongly perceived as a Marxist strain in their thinking, and increasingly sensitive to any criticism as the burdens of the Harvard deanship weighed heavily upon him. After stepping down from law school administration in 1936, Pound developed other reasons to despise the realists. In the main, he found fault with them for their enthusiastic support of Franklin Roosevelt and the New Deal. For a lifelong Republican and critic of a strong executive department, this was too much to bear quietly.[64] Also, when Pound wrote his 1931 law review article, he may have had on his mind two recently published books authored by prominent younger scholars, *The Bramble Bush*[65] by Llewellyn and *Law and the Modern Mind*[66] by Jerome Frank. Both books were highly critical of conventional, precedent-bound legal thinking. Frank's book, moreover, highlighted some of Pound's views for criticism as being deluded by "the myth of legal certainty."[67]

Believing that Pound's criticisms had been directed largely at them, Llewellyn and Frank set to work on a rejoinder, which they published in the *Harvard Law Review* under the title "Some Realism About Realism—Responding to Dean Pound."[68] Llewellyn's hand "pushed the pen" for the article, but Frank collaborated on the first part of it. The article is a brilliant piece of scholarly overkill. It takes issue with Pound's vague charges against the realists, granting them perhaps more dignity and clarity than they deserve, and then disposes of them ruthlessly and exhaustively. The prose is terse and polemical; compared to Llewellyn's usual jerry-built diction and convoluted style, the writing in "Some Realism About Realism" is a model of clarity and precision.

The first part of the article takes Pound's charges against the "younger teachers," carefully groups them, and then attempts to show that they have little if any factual basis. Llewellyn put the matter this way near the beginning of the essay:

The question is one of fact: whether the offenses have been committed. For if they have, the Dean's rebukes are needed. Spare the rod and spoil the realist. The question is one of fact. By fact it must be tried. And tried it must be.[69]

Since Pound named no specific individuals as falling prey to his charges Llewellyn and Frank compiled a list of those scholars whom they believed were the most important of the "new realists." They then surveyed the published writings of the twenty men whom they listed as leading realists, finding that virtually none of them fell prey to Pound's criticisms.[70]

Llewellyn went on in the second part of the article—now speaking only for himself—and laid down nine "common points of departure" for the twenty realists. His nine points can be distilled to the following propositions. He contended that the realists as a group saw the law and society in flux, interacting at various points. Because society was typically in flux faster than law, Llewellyn contended that the realists believed the law demanded a searching reexamination. This reexamination required a distrust of traditional legal rules, concepts, and theories about how the law works or should work. To undertake the necessary reexamination, a "temporary" divorce or "Is" and "Ought" was essential for purposes of study. Finally, the ensuing study, Llewellyn submitted, should involve a description of what legal agencies actually do and a focus on the demonstrable effects of the law.[71] Llewellyn's summary of the realists' basic premises has its weaknesses and lacunae, of course,[72] but it does offer an early, cogent précis of realist thinking, composed by a sympathetic participant rather than a hostile critic. Although Llewellyn insisted that the realists were not a group or a school,[73] the legal community as a whole often thought of them as such after the publication of the Llewellyn-Frank article. Thus, no *realist movement* may have existed in any programmatic or organizational sense, but after the appearance of "Some Realism About Realism," the term achieved a wide degree of currency and was stamped, for better or for worse, upon certain individuals.

Realism after 1931

To answer the question "Who were the realists?" most scholars have looked first to the 1931 list of twenty names compiled by

Llewellyn and Frank.[74] This list may suit every student of American legal history, but the choices subsume a range of individuals whose published ideas and attitudes properly express the great diversity of the realist movement. The leaders of the campaign for a functional curriculum at Columbia in the late twenties—Underhill Moore, Herman Oliphant, and Hessel Yntema—were on the list; so were three of the most devoted empirical legal researchers at Yale in the early thirties—William O. Douglas, Charles Clark, and Wesley Sturges. Llewellyn and Frank also included themselves, principally because of their recent writings and their self-appointed role as cataloguers of the movement; Judge Hutcheson, largely because of his article on the role of the hunch in judicial decision making; Walter Wheeler Cook, for his advocacy of empirical legal research and his role in founding the Institute of Law at Johns Hopkins; and Arthur Corbin, for his intellectual leadership of the movement.[75] Interestingly, sixteen of the men named on the Llewellyn-Frank list had, in the late twenties and early thirties, close connections with either the Yale or Columbia law schools or, in a few cases, with both. All but three were born between 1878 and 1901. In spite of the deficiencies in the Llewellyn-Frank list,[76] it represents a fair attempt at sampling the movement. After all, Llewellyn and Frank were not trying to present a definitive prosopography of realism; they were merely writing a polemical article. They were probably correct in submitting that this sample recognized elements of the realist movement both "characteristic and extreme."[77]

Having traversed the history of twentieth-century American legal philosophy up to and including the Pound-Llewellyn exchange in 1930-31, a large portion of the journey to understand legal realism is complete. After 1931 the realists continued to write and speak and teach, emphasizing the need to be skeptical of the validity of legal rules and theories, the need to examine the legal experience in terms of what actually happens rather than what should or is supposed to occur, the need to bring law and the other social sciences more into alignment, and the need to perform empirical legal research to procure the necessary information for an accurate description and ultimate assessment of the legal process. In the thirties, various realists, their sympathizers, and their critics wrote hundreds of articles on these themes in the major law school journals.[78] However, it would serve little purpose to review the points raised in this literature because most of the lines of analysis had been set out before 1931.

Until the Pound-Llewellyn exchange, the principal commentary surrounding legal realism involved the curricular innovations at Columbia, the role of empirical legal research championed by various members of the faculties at Columbia, Yale, Johns Hopkins, and even Harvard, and the skepticism toward legal rules highlighted in books such as *The Bramble Bush* and *Law and the Modern Mind*. One critic of realism whimsically referred to the early stages of the movement as a "play-off for the Ivy League championship, with the combined faculties of the Columbia and Yale Law Schools taking the field against Harvard."[79] Until the early thirties, realism can be identified with a few elite institutions and a few law professors, but by the end of the decade, the "movement" was no longer so narrowly confined. The gospel of realism was carried from the Ivy League to the hinterlands. Hutchins took many of the realists' ideas with him to the University of Chicago, where he was instrumental in inaugurating a four-year curriculum in the Law School that included courses in psychology, English constitutional history, economic theory, and ethics.[80] Likewise, the University of Wisconsin Law School was, by the middle of the thirties, engaged in the same type of curricular and research matters that had occupied the Ivy League professors a few years earlier.[81] But in all likelihood, the most pronounced national impact of the realist movement was in the widespread use by scores of law schools of the "cases and materials" texts. A book such as Jerome Michael and Herbert Wechsler's *Cases and Materials on Criminal Law and Its Administration* was used as an effective teaching tool and provided good propaganda for the realists' social science orientation.[82] Even a 1,100 page tome such as Llewellyn's *Cases and Materials on Sales,* which contained pages and pages of extra-legal materials and information and was generally considered too demanding and too lengthy for students, did have a definite influence on the law teaching profession as a piece of scholarship.[83]

Just as legal philosophy earlier in the century was affected by events and the general climate of opinion, so too was the realism of the thirties. Legal realism seemed particularly well-suited to the mood of the Depression and the New Deal. The Depression called into question a number of American verities, among them the conviction that a loosely regulated capitalist system could survive unscathed any economic hardship. The realist who could, with unsentimental skepticism, reject what Jerome Frank characterized as the "basic legal myth"—that is, the notion that legal doctrine is settled and certain[84]—was at home in the thirties. Such a realist was committed to facts rather than theories, willing to engage in detailed empirical research to unearth the roots of a problem, and then able to propose solutions untinged by obsolete ideas. As one recent scholar noted:

The times called, in law, as in all other areas, for hardheaded realism derived from sharp and relentless analysis of the facts. . . .[85]

It is no accident that the realists became favorite problem solvers in the New Deal. President Roosevelt relied heavily on the quasi-realist Felix Frankfurter as a talent scout for the selection of individuals for high positions in the federal government. Douglas was appointed to the Securities and Exchange Commission and later to the Supreme Court; Dean Clark of Yale was appointed to the court of appeals; Jerome Frank served as the General Counsel to the Agricultural Adjustment Administration, as an SEC commissioner, and as a court of appeals judge; and Thurman Arnold served in the Agricultural Adjustment Administration, at various capacities in the Department of Justice, and was appointed a court of appeals judge. Realism was particularly compatible with what has been called the "First New Deal,"[86] the period of experimentation and bold federal legislation in Roosevelt's first administration. Later, realist arguments were employed to uncover the biases of the conservative members of the Supreme Court who voted to strike down some of the most fundamental and innovative pieces of New Deal legislation. In his 1941 book, *The Struggle for Judicial Supremacy*, Robert Jackson—Roosevelt's Attorney General in 1937 when the President's bill to add memebrs to the Supreme Court was proposed—argued that the protest against the philosophy of Supreme Court decisions such as *Schecter Poultry* v. *U.S.*[87] and *U.S.* v. *Butler*[88] was led by "influential spokesmen . . . in our universities distinguished for disinterested legal scholarship."[89] Although Jackson named no specific spokesman as critics of the Court's majority views, he was no doubt alluding to some of the realists who were on the record in favor of the ill-starred, "court-packing" legislation.

Realism and the Penchant for Information

A recapitulation of some of the views of selected realists places in stark relief the crucial dimension that information and empirical study held for the realists. In truth, the penchant for information reached its height with the realist movement. Seen in this light, realism was the logical and historical outcome of a legal generation's emphasis on information. The stress here is placed upon the actions of realists and not their rhetoric—a notion consistent with a cardinal principal of realism.

The clearest manifestation of the informational paradigm in the activities of the realists was their empirical research. Primarily under the auspices of the Johns Hopkins Institute of Law and the Yale University Law School, individuals generally recognized as realists engaged in the most rigorous empirical legal studies ever undertaken by American scholars. At the Institute of Law, Leon Marshall and his associates collected what was then an unprecedented amount of data on the administration of justice in the United States. Some of the data was presented for the perusal of the legal community in published volumes such as Marshall's *Unlocking the Treasuries of the Trial Courts*. Regrettably, the short life and abrupt demise of the Institute meant that the numerous projected studies were not undertaken. When the Institute ceased operating due to lack of funding, its scholars were just beginning to move beyond the mere assembling of the data into the more crucial stages of analysis and synthesis. At the Yale Law School, however—in conjunction with Hutchins's Institute for Human Relations—empirical legal research reached a more sophisticated stage. Dean Clark's studies of judicial administration, the work directed by Douglas on bankruptcies, and, most importantly, Underhill Moore's empirical and behavioral studies offered the most impressive published results of the realists' penchant for information. Moore's research on overtime parking seemed trivial to some sectors of the legal community, but it must be said that no legal scholar of his generation understood as clearly as did Moore the proper relationship between behavioral theory and empirical research. To complete the summary of data-centered legal research, mention should be made of the research of Pound on crime and Frankfurter and Landis on the business of the Supreme Court. Because these three men were ensconced at Harvard did not mean that they were not touched by some currents of realism.

Besides the empirical bent of realist research, the law teaching of many of the realists was influenced by their lust for data. The functional reformers at Columbia in the late twenties injected much extra-legal information into their new courses—principally legislative history and bits of economics, business administration and sociology. Although the functionalists' attempt to found a new model for legal education has to be judged a failure, many of their ideas were and still are being carried on in multidisciplinary casebooks. The volume usually considered to be the first of these casebooks—*Cases and Materials on Sales*—was put together by the Columbia professor and leading realist, Karl Llewellyn, and a volume often praised as the best of this genre—*Materials on Criminal Law and Its Administration*—was assembled by Jerome Michael, a young professor at Columbia in the late twenties, and Herbert Wechsler, a Columbia law student from 1928 to 1931. Scores of the multidisciplinary casebooks were compiled in the thirties and early forties. In large part, it was the spread of such casebooks from Columbia and Yale to law schools across the country that kept realism from being merely a parochial fad of the Ivy League. It should be added, too, that a few of the professors sympathetic to the empirical dimension of realism sent their own law students off to conduct individually designed empirical research; this occurred mainly at Yale where the relatively small classes lent themselves to such individually tailored projects.

Any discussion of legal realism cannot be regarded as satisfactory without special commentary on the views of the two most well-known and controversial members of the movement, Karl Llewellyn and Jerome Frank. Neither could be said to have been enamored of empirical research, but both had a feel for the importance of extra-legal materials and influences on the law.

Even before Llewellyn attended law school, he achieved a minor distinction as being the only American citizen decorated by the German Army in World War I. This is a story in itself.[90] After being abruptly mustered out of the service, Llewellyn returned to the United States to finish an undergraduate degree at Yale College and then attended the Yale Law School. While a law student, he fell under the influence of Arthur Corbin and Wesley Hohfeld. He taught in the Yale Law School in the early twenties and came to Columbia in 1927, where he remained until 1951. Llewellyn's first legal interest was commercial law, which ultimately led to his position as the Reporter for the Uniform Commercial Code (UCC). But Llewellyn also commanded a specialty in jurisprudence. His writings on realism in the thirties and forties made him, perhaps, as well known as a legal philosopher as an expert on commercial law. Besides his monumental labors for the UCC and his polemics for realism, Llewellyn is remembered for his collaboration with anthropologist E. Adamson Hoebel on a path-breaking study of American Indian law.[91]

Llewellyn's view of empirical research is summarized in a little known law review article, "The Theory of Legal Science," published in 1941.[92] Essentially, Llewellyn argued in the article that the empirical description of phenomena was essential for the development of a legal science. This corresponded with his view, expressed a decade earlier in "Some Realism About Realism," to the effect that legal analysis should abjure the "paper rules" and both seek a description of what courts and people actually do and search out the observable effects of legal rules.[93] Llewellyn favored a multiplicity of modest programs of empirical research over and against expensive, macroprojects. He participated in some of the field work for *The Cheyenne Way*, but he was not personally an enthusiastic data gatherer. He was, though, a helpful advisor of the empirical work of others. Some of his graduate students produced excellent empirical studies under his direction. Also, his *Cases and Materials on Sales* was a masterful job of scissors and paste that dutifully included some material derived from empirical studies. In short, even though Llewellyn had little taste for performing empirical research himself, he acknowledged the need for more data-oriented legal research, recognized and paid proper respect to it in reviews, his teaching, and his casebooks, and defended such studies in his polemical articles.

Jerome Frank,[94] like Llewellyn, cannot be considered a devoted empiricist. But the thrust of some of his most important observations on the legal process are, nonetheless, consistent with the informational penchant. Frank, unlike Llewellyn, was not primarily a law professor. He did teach a course from time to time at the Yale Law School, but most of his legal activity involved his law practice and later his government service in a variety of roles, including that of an appeals court judge. Frank received his legal training at the University of Chicago Law School. After graduation he practiced law in Chicago and New York. His first book, *Law and the Modern Mind*, created a legal sensation. It was reviewed by over thirty periodicals, and it quickly became one of the essential statements of the realist viewpoint. In *Law and the Modern Mind*, Frank set forth an avowedly psychoanalytical interpretation of the law's overwhelming fixation with certainty and predictability.[95] In his 1930 volume, Frank also introduced a theme that he would come back to again and again throughout his career as a writer, bureaucrat, and judge: that the crucial stage in any legal proceeding is the fact-finding stage and that facts are never certain, dependent on a variety of subjective and nonquantifiable influences.

This "fact-skepticism," as Frank preferred to call it, was the basis for his view of the judicial process. Frank was critical of anyone, including realists such as Llewellyn, who seemed more concerned with the activities of appellate courts and their precedents than with the "act" of fact finding at the trial court level. He referred to the delusion of these misguided thinkers as "upper-courtitis."[96] Other realists, such as Moore and Douglas, attempted to get as close to the facts in a legal situation as possible by engaging in empirical research. Frank should properly be regarded as a sympathetic critic of their efforts. His clearest statement on the problems with empirical inquiry is found in a chapter of his book, *Courts on Trial: Myth and Reality in American Justice*,[97] a compendium of Frank's most illuminating ideas on the judicial process, many of which had appeared earlier in the form of law review articles. After devoting several pages to a criticism of various attempts at data gathering and the creation of a "legal science," Frank acknowledges that a rejection of the notion of the eventual accession of a science of the law does not mean that it is necessary to turn one's back on the products of scientific inquiry or on what Frank terms the "scientific spirit." He supports the need for empirical research but cautions that the scientific spirit demands:

> . . . the discipline of suspended judgment; the rigorous weighing of all the evidence; a consideration of all possible theories; the questioning of the plausible, of the respectably accepted and seemingly self-evident; a serene passion for verification; what I would call "constructive skepticism" . . . plus an eagerness not to be deceived.[98]

This is a credo that even a devoted legal field researcher like Underhill Moore could have endorsed.

Moreover, Frank himself was not opposed to borrowing useful social science theories to support his idiosyncratic generalizations. For example, he employed Jean Piaget's model of children's thoughtways to support his belief that many people regard the law as children regard their fathers,[99] and he applied the notion of patterns in Gestalt psychology to the practice of trial court decision making.[100] By finding such theories useful to his own examination of the law, Frank was implicitly relying upon the empirical data upon which those theories depend. Frank may have been a skeptic, but he was not a nihilist.

Realism and the penchant for information existed in symbiosis. Realism could not have flourished as it did during the interwar years without an empirical component. A realist like Underhill Moore, an enthusiastic field worker, was literally consumed by data. However, even the more well-known skeptics, Karl Llewellyn and Jerome Frank, operated within the informational paradigm. The penchant for information reached its zenith under the realist movement, but when realism went into eclipse during World War II, so too did the penchant for information.

Notes

1. The exchange is found in three law review articles: Karl Llewellyn, "A Realistic Jurisprudence—The Next Step," 30 *Columbia Law Review* 431 (1930); Roscoe Pound, "The Call for a Realistic Jurisprudence," 44 *Harvard Law Review* 697 (1931); and Llewellyn, "Some Realism About Realism—Responding to Dean Pound," 44 *Harvard Law Review* 1222 (1931).

2. The best discussions of realism include Wilfrid E. Rumble, Jr., *American Legal Realism: Skepticism, Reform, and the Judicial Process* (Ithaca, N.Y., 1968); Eugene V. Rostow, "The Realist Tradition in American Law," in Arthur Schlesinger, Jr., and Morton White, eds., *Paths of American Thought* (Boston, 1963), pp. 203-218; William Twining, *Karl Llewellyn and the Realist Movement* (London, 1973), pp. 3-83, 375-387, et passim; Edward A. Purcell, Jr., "American Jurisprudence Between the Wars: Legal Realism and the Crisis of Democratic Theory," 75 *American Historical Review* 424 (1969); Calvin Woodard, "The Limits of Legal Realism: A Historical Perspective," 54 *Virginia Law Review* 689 (1968) [reprinted in Herbert L. Packer and Thomas Ehrlich, eds., *New Directions in Legal Education* (New York, 1972), pp. 331-384]; G. Edward White, "Sociological Jurisprudence to Realism: Jurisprudence and Social Change in Early Twentieth Century America," 58 *Virginia Law Review* 999 (1972); and White, "The Evolution of Reasoned Elaboration: Jurisprudential Criticism and Social Change," 59 *Virginia Law Review* 279 (1973) [the two articles by White are reprinted in his *Patterns of American Legal Thought* (Indianapolis, 1978), pp. 99-163]. Older discussions of realism, more contemporary to the movement itself, are noted in Rumble, pp. 1-3, note 1. The realists have not yet benefited from a first-rate, comprehensive prosopography. Twining's treatment of realism is, to my mind, the best available.

3. Twining, xi.

4. See G. Edward White, "The Rise and Fall of Justice Holmes" 39 *University of Chicago Law Review* 51 (1971) [reprinted in White, *Patterns of American Legal Thought*, pp. 194-226] for different assessments of Holmes as a philosopher and a judge.

5. Oliver Wendell Holmes, *The Common Law* (Boston, 1881).

6. Some of Holmes's most famous philosophical statements are found in Max Lerner, ed., *The Mind and Faith of Justice Holmes: His Speeches, Essays, Letters and Judicial Opinions* (New York, 1943); collections of Holmes's voluminous correspondence include Mark DeWolfe Howe, ed., *The Holmes-Pollock Letters*, 2 vols. (Cambridge, Mass., 1941) and Howe, ed., *The Holmes-Laski Letters*, 2 vols. (Cambridge, Mass., 1953). See also Oliver Wendell Holmes, *Collected Legal Papers* (Washington, 1920).

7. Benjamin N. Cardozo, "Mr. Justice Holmes" 44 *Harvard Law Review* 682, 691 (1933).

8. Karl Llewellyn, quoted in John T. Noonan, Jr., *Persons and Masks of the Law: Cardozo, Holmes, Jefferson, and Wythe as Makers of the Masks* (New York, 1976), p. 67.

9. *The Common Law*, p. 1

10. Holmes, *Collected Legal Papers*, pp. 172-173.

11. "Rarely has so vast an influence been built upon so slight a body of legal writing. Perhaps because of the very slenderness of the text and the gnomic quality of its utterances, each commentator has seen in Holmes something different, and generally something to suit his own preconceptions." Lerner, p. 367.

12. See, for example, Jerome Frank, *Law and the Modern Mind* (New York, 1930), pp. 253-260; and Karl Llewellyn, *The Bramble Bush: Some Lectures on Law and Its Study* (New York, 1930), ix.

13. Morton White, *Social Thought in America: The Revolt Against Formalism* (Boston, 1949), pp. 15-18, 59-75, et passim.

14. Ibid., pp. 11-46.

15. Ibid., p. 236.

16. Howe, *Holmes-Laski Letters*, I, pp. 204-205.

17. 213 U.S. 347 (1909).

18. Ibid., 351-359.

19. This discussion of Holmes's opinion in *American Banana Company* v. *United Fruit Company* is drawn largely from John Noonan's brilliant little book, *Persons and Masks of the Law*, pp. 65-110.

20. Frank, pp. 253-260.

21. Pound's most famous article critical of the realists in his "The Call for a Realistic Jurisprudence," 44 *Harvard Law Review* 697 (1931). On Pound's aversion to realism generally, see David Wigdor, *Roscoe Pound: Philosopher of Law* (Westport, Conn., 1974), pp. 255-277.

22. 8 *Columbia Law Review* 605 (1908).

23. 44 *American Law Review* 12 (1910).

24. 19 *Green Bag* 607 (1907).

25. On Pound's career, see generally Wigdor. See also Twining, pp. 22-24; Arthur Sutherland, *The Law at Harvard: A History of Ideas and Men, 1817-1967* (Cambridge, Mass., 1967), pp. 236-240; and Rumble, pp. 9-15.

26. Roscoe Pound, "Liberty of Contract," 18 *Yale Law Journal* 454, 464 (1909).

27. See Pound, "The Need of a Sociological Jurisprudence," 19 *Green Bag* 607, 611-612.

28. See Purcell, "American Jurisprudence Between the Wars," 427.

29. Wigdor, in his biography of Pound, attempts to explain this apparent anomaly in Pound's thought by suggesting that Pound's legal philosophy consisted of an "unresolved dualism" of competing elements of "organicism" and "instrumentalism." Wigdor, pp. 207-232.

30. 37 *Harvard Law Review* 933 (1924).

31. Twining, p. 24.

32. See Wigdor, pp. 233-281; and Seligman, *The High Citadel: The Influence of Harvard Law School* (Boston, 1978), pp. 57-67.

33. Seligman, p. 66.

34. See Twining, pp. 20-22, 26-37.

35. Samuel J. Konefsky, *The Legacy of Holmes and Brandeis: A Study in the History of Ideas* (New York, 1956), p. 92.

36. On the relationship between sociological jurisprudence and Progressivism, see the very thoughtful discussion of G. Edward White, *Patterns of American Legal Thought*, pp. 100-115.

37. See Robert H. Bremner, *From the Depths: The Discovery of Poverty in the United States* (New York, 1956), pp. 140-163. On the Progressive Movement generally, see Samuel Hays, *The Response to Industrialization, 1885-1914* (Chicago, 1957), pp. 48-62; and Robert H. Wiebe, *The Search for Order, 1877-1920* (New York, 1967), pp. 76 223.

38. Quoted in Bremner, p. 154.

39. See generally Clarke A. Chambers, *Paul U. Kellogg and the Survey: Voices for Social Welfare and Social Justice* (Minneapolis, 1971) See also Bremner, pp. 154-157; and Clarke A. Chambers, *Seedtime of Reform: American Social Service and Social Action, 1918-1933* (Minneapolis, 1963), pp. 261-262.

40. See William E. Leuchtenburg, *The Perils of Prosperity, 1914-1932* (Chicago, 1958), pp. 126-127; and Leslie Fishbein, "Righteousness, Romance, Sex Drives, Hard Cash: Changing Views of Prostitution, 1870-1920" (Unpublished paper, delivered at the Annual Meeting of the Organization of American Historians, Atlanta, 1977).

41. 35 *Harvard Law Review* 489 (1912).

42. Ibid., 515.

43. Holmes, *Collected Legal Papers*, pp. 172-174.

44. On the effect of World War I on the climate of opinion among American intellectuals, see esp. Leuchtenburg, pp. 140-177, 204-224.

45. See Arthur Link, "What Happened to the Progressive Movement in the Twenties?" 64 *American Historical Review* 833 (1959).

46. See Wigdor, pp. 233-254.

47. Charles Grove Haines, "General Observations on the Effects of Personal, Political, and Economic Influences in the Decisions of Judges," 17 *Illinois Law Review* 96 (1922).

48. See also Max Radin, "The Theory of Judicial Decision: Or How Judges Think," 11 *American Bar Association Journal* 357 (1925).

49. Benjamin N. Cardozo, *The Nature of the Judicial Process* (New Haven, 1921), p. 167.

50. Joseph Hutcheson, "The Judgment Intuitive: The Function of the 'Hunch' in Judicial Decision," 14 *Cornell Law Quarterly* 274 (1929).

51. Julius Goebel, Jr., et al., *A History of the School of Law, Columbia University* (New York, 1955), pp. 275-305.

52. William Twining believes to the contrary. In his view, the realist movement started to diffuse with the 1928 schism at Columbia. See Twining pp. 67-69, 377.

53. Twining offers the Bloomsbury Group model as a description of the intellectual friendships in the Yale Law School faculty of the World War I years. Twining, p. 26. In actuality, the notion of a Bloomsbury Group more accurately describes the Columbia law faculty of the late twenties or the Yale law faculty of the thirties.

54. 30 *Columbia Law Review* 431 (1930).

55. Ibid., 464.

56. "The more one learns, the more one studies, the more light and stimulus Pound's writing gives. But always peculiarly on a fringe of insight which fails to penetrate at all to the more systematic set-up of the material." Ibid., 435, note 3.

57. Pound "The Call for a Realistic Jurisprudence," 44 *Harvard Law Review* 697 (1931).

58. The article was written, by Pound's own admission, while he was preoccupied by administrative matters at the Harvard Law School and with his work as a member of the National Commission on Law Observation and Enforcement. Twining, p. 72.

59. Pound, "The Call for a Realistic Jurisprudence," 697.

60. Ibid., 701.

61. Ibid., 700.

62. Ibid., 707.

63. See Rumble, pp. 13-20.

64. On Pound's attitudes toward legal realism and the New Deal, see Wigdor, pp. 249-274.

65. (New York, 1930).

66. Frank, *Law and the Modern Mind*.

67. Ibid., pp. 207-216.

68. Karl Llewellyn and Jerome Frank, "Some Realism About Realism—Responding to Dean Pound," 44 *Harvard Law Review* 1222 (1931).

69. Ibid., 1225.

70. Ibid., 1237.

71. Ibid., 1233-1256.

72. Twining, for example, criticizes Llewellyn's account of realism for its failure to "analyse the ideas of a rather variegated selection of people

without reference to the relevant historical background, the institutional context, or the specific issues that agitated them." Twining, p. 80.

73. Llewellyn and Frank, "Some Realism About Realism," 1234, 1256.

74. Ibid., 1226-1227, note 18.

75. The other nine named by Llewellyn and Frank were Thomas R. Powell, Joseph W. Bingham, Leon Green, Samuel Klaus, E.G. Lorenzen, Edwin Patterson, L.A. Tulin, Max Radin and Joseph F. Francis. Ibid., 1226-1227, note 18.

76. As a complete roster of the realist movement, the Llewellyn-Frank list leaves much to be desired. It may have been acceptable for the polemical purpose of disputing Pound's views to confine the list to "younger teachers," but an intellectually and historically accurate list would have had to include older men and even some who had died before the term "realism" became fashionable: Holmes, Wesley Hohfeld, John Chipman Gray, Brandeis, and even Pound himself would have had to be included in such a group. Also the Llewellyn-Frank list ignores the place of nonlaw trained scholars in the movement such as business professor Leon Marshall of Columbia and Johns Hopkins and psychologists Mortimer Adler of Columbia and Edwin Robinson of Yale. For no apparent reason, the list ignores Adolph A. Berle and Julius Goebel of Columbia and Thurman Arnold and Walton Hamilton of Yale. The list, of course, does not acknowledge the place among the realists of individuals who became identified with the movement after 1931, for example, Robert Hutchins, Fred Rodell, and Myres McDougal—all of Yale, and Jerome Michael of Columbia. Finally, the Harvard stalwart, Felix Frankfurter, was not included in the 1931 sample because Llewellyn and Frank accepted without question Frankfurter's own designation of himself as a sociological jurisprudent and not a realist. See the comments on composing a list of realists in Twining, pp. 75-77, and pp. 409-410, notes 22 and 23; Purcell, "American Jurisprudence Between the Wars," 427-428, note 9; Llewellyn, "Some Realism About Realism," 1226-1227, note 18.

77. Llewellyn, "Some Realism About Realism," 1227, note 18.

78. For bibliographies of the writings of the realists, see Llewellyn, "Some Realism About Realism," 1257-1259; Rumble, pp. 1-3, note 1; pp. 22-23, note 44; pp. 29-30, note 53; p. 32, note 56; p. 65, note 30; pp. 99-100, note 94; pp. 156-157, note 40; p. 162, note 45; p. 184, note 1; p. 234, note 80. See also Twining, pp. 475-476, notes 4 and 5, pp. 555-561.

79. Grant Gilmore offered this tongue-in-cheek characterization of William Twining's account of the realist movement. See Gilmore, *The Ages of American Law* (New Haven, 1977), p. 78.

80. Robert Stevens, "Two Cheers for 1870: The American Law School," 5 *Perspectives in American History* 405, 484-485 (1971).

81. William R. Johnson, *Schooled Lawyers: A Study in the Clash of Professional Cultures* (New York, 1978), pp. 168-169.

82. See the discussion of the "cases and materials" texts, *supra*, chapter 6. See also Albert Ehrenzweig, "The American Casebook: 'Cases and Materials' " 32 *Georgetown Law Journal* 224 (1944); and David Riesman, "Law and Social Science: A Report on Michael and Wechsler's Classbook on Criminal Law and Administration," 50 *Yale Law Journal* 636 (1940).

83. Twining, p. 131.

84. See Frank, pp. 3-21, et passim.

85. Paul L. Murphy, *The Constitution in Crisis Times, 1918-1969* (New York, 1972), p. 99.

86. See Purcell, "American Jurisprudence Between the Wars," 436-437; White, *Patterns of American Legal Thought*, pp. 139-140. On the "First New Deal," see Arthur Schlesinger, Jr., *The Coming of the New Deal* (Boston, 1958), pp. 179-194, et passim; and William Leuchtenburg, *Franklin D. Roosevelt and the New Deal* (New York, 1963), pp. 41-117.

87. 295 U.S. 495 (1935).

88. 297 U.S. 1 (1936).

89. Robert Jackson, *The Struggle for Judicial Supremacy* (New York, 1941), v.

90. This unusual story is told by Twining, pp. 479-487. Twining's biography is the definitive work on Llewellyn and is easily the best biography of any of the leading realists.

91. Karl Llewellyn and Adamson Hoebel, *The Cheyenne Way* (Norman, Okla., 1941). Llewellyn participated in field work on the law of other Indian tribes. However, the results of those studies were never published.

92. 20 *North Carolina Law Review* 1 (1941). See also Twining, pp. 188-196.

93. Llewellyn, "Some Realism About Realism," 1237.

94. The best biography of Jerome Frank is Julius Paul, *The Legal Realism of Jerome Frank* (The Hague, 1959).

95. See Frank, pp. 3-21, 100-117, et passim.

96. Jerome Frank, *Courts on Trial: Myth and Reality in American Justice* (Princeton, 1949), pp. 222-224.

97. Ibid., pp. 190-221.

98. Ibid., p. 219.

99. Frank, *Law and the Modern Mind*, pp. 69-75.

100. Frank, *Courts on Trial*, pp. 165-185.

8
THE PENCHANT FOR
INFORMATION IN
ECLIPSE

The face of American legal culture has changed dramatically since 1940. It would be impossible in a few short pages to trace out all of the new lines in the visage of American law. However, one thing is clear: the penchant for information went into decline about forty years ago and has never regained the vitality it enjoyed in the 1930s. This is not to say that all aspects of the informational paradigm have been subdued in the last generation. For example, the judicial citation of extra-legal information was well institutionalized by 1940 and did not decline after World War II. The U.S. Supreme Court's rate of citing extra-legal materials, which had jumped significantly in the late 1930s, sustained "no dramatic increases or decreases" between 1940 and 1970.[1] Certainly, courts today are forced to contend with more reams of technical information than ever before, the current IBM antitrust action being the most visible case in point. Yet, in the face of indications that extra-legal information is still very much alive in the country's legal culture, the high degree of faith that the 1908-40 American legal community placed in such information has been absent since World War II.

Since 1940 no champion of factual information in the legal process has arisen to rival the early twentieth-century role of Louis Brandeis. Although compilations of information on the law such as the Restatement and *American Jurisprudence* are still being published, no new massive repositories of legal information have been founded since the early 1940s. Judges still rely upon legislative history as much today as they did in the 1930s, but the passion for searching out legislative intent from collateral sources has been on the wane for some time. Recent commentators on constitutional and statutory interpretation have argued that legislative history should be only one guide in the construction of controversial language.[2] Law professors still assign "cases and materials" texts to their students, but the goal of integrating the social sciences into legal education is now a shopworn cliché that is seldom taken seriously any more by legal educators. At virtually the same time that the Association of American Law Schools was holding its 1969 annual meeting on the theme "Social Research and the Law," law professor turned sociologist David Riesman commented that "in most universities the law schools have remained autarchic, sharing only the most nominal connections with . . . education in the arts and sciences." Two years earlier, the Law Students Association at Yale University—the major American law school that through the years has been the most committed to instruction in the social sciences—found the often articulated promise of interdisciplinary activity in the Law School "largely unfulfilled."[3] And the legal realist movement, a diffuse but intensive effort on the part of a number of law professors who strongly supported empirical inquiry into legal subjects, is now defunct and in many quarters discredited. Realism exists today only to the extent that the legal community generally accepts the realists' skepticism regarding certainty in the law and their distrust of "paper rules." For the last generation or more, law professors have been repeating a curious epigram: "realism is dead; we are all realists."[4] Understood properly, this is a classic example of damning with faint praise.

Empiricism on the Wane

What, then, happened to the commitment to information that was so pronounced in American legal culture in the 1930s? For one thing, the advocates of empirical research into legal subjects claimed too much for their work. They raised to the heights expectations of significant substantive findings. When the dramatic results were not quickly forthcoming, some of the enthusiasm of the early partisans of empirical research was lost and the antagonism of its critics was intensified. Robert Hutchins, for example, had been a sympathetic supporter of social science research while at the Yale Law School in the late 1920s. While dean of the Law School, he had recruited social scientists for the faculty and had spearheaded the fund-raising drive for the interdisciplinary Institute of Human Relations. Yet, by 1934 his faith in the social sciences had soured. In an article published in the first volume of the *University of Chicago Law Review*, Hutchins reported that:

From their disciplines as such the social scientists added little or nothing. . . . The fact was that though the social scientists seemed to have a great deal of information, we could not see and they could not tell us how to use it.[5]

One of the reasons the social sciences failed to deliver payoffs in the realm of legal research is that they were, in the 1930s, in a state of infancy. Crude empiricism, without carefully articulated theory, seemed to be the order of the day. Hutchins again put the matter succinctly:

Empirical operations do not make a science. Facts do not organize themselves. . . . [w]e must accumulate cases, facts, and data. I simply insist that we must have a scheme into which to fit them.[6]

It is no wonder, given statements such as these, that the work of the Johns Hopkins Institute failed to excite the legal profession as a whole. The researchers there were so busy gathering data that they did not take time out to ask what their numbers meant.

Besides the disillusionment of the true believers, the movement to engage in social science research into legal subjects was frustrated by the activities of those who were unsympathetic from the beginning. The Columbia Law School's functional curriculum had a very short period of hegemony—only about two years—partly because traditionalists on the faculty resisted the efforts of the social scientifically-oriented professors. Moreover, even Roscoe Pound, a man who engaged in social science research himself in the early twenties, resisted any attempt to found a social science track of courses at the Harvard Law School during his deanship. Since the late nineteenth century, most American law schools have looked to Harvard for direction in curricular design and teaching methods: so when Harvard refused to grant serious consideration in the twenties and early thirties to the social sciences, most other institutions followed suit. Although empirical legal studies were continued well into the thirties by members of the Yale faculty, they did not flourish at any other law schools. Even if the willingness had existed elsewhere, few law schools in the Depression could have afforded the apparent luxury of intellectual research that offered no immediate practical benefits. Nor could many law schools attract outside funding for such endeavors.

Thus, a combination of factors led to the demise of empirical legal research in the late 1930s: unsophisticated social science methodology, the antagonism of critics and traditional legal educators who thought such research took too much time and energy away from the practical training of attorneys, the disillusionment of true believers, and the unhospitable financial climate of the decade. With the exception of Underhill Moore's research on law and learning theory that continued into the 1940s, empirical legal research virtually vanished from the law schools near the beginning of World War II.[7] Only in the 1960s, after a hiatus of about a quarter century, did influential members of the legal community once again concern themselves seriously with empirical studies.[8]

The "Death" of Legal Realism

The rapid falling away of interest in empirical legal research was part of a larger phenomenon affecting the legal community in the late 1930s and early 1940s. Legal realism, a movement that had from its inception been assailed by vitriolic criticism, was placed on the defensive near the end of the 1930s and virtually decimated during the war years. The death of realism served to drive one more very large spike into the coffin of the informational paradigm.

Many of the advocates of what came to be called "legal realism" emphasized that legal research should not be predicated upon the values of the researchers. Llewellyn, for example, argued that a cardinal principle of realism was "the temporary divorce of Is and Ought for the purpose of study."[9] Further, Llewellyn maintained that researchers should concern themselves primarily with the observable behavior of legal actors and that "the rules and precepts and principles . . . should be displaced."[10] Llewellyn made these comments in articles published in 1930 and 1931. It is fair to say that most of the empirically minded realists of the early thirties agreed with Llewellyn on these points.[11] However, in the second half of the decade, criticism of realism for its ethical relativism reached flood tide, and many of the realists themselves were swept along in the wake of moral absolutism.

By 1935 worldwide totalitarianism had placed American legal realism on the defensive, and, as the decade rushed to a close in the horror of a world war, realism was dealt a series of heavy blows from which it never recovered.[12] American intellectuals, recoiling in outrage at the Stalinist purges, the atrocities of Franco and Mussolini, and the naked "might-makes-right" philosophy of Nazi Germany, struck out at legal realism. How, the critics asked, in the face of such brutal tyranny, could a group of American scholars downplay the role of values and moral principles? How, they charged, could realists assert that the stark behavior of men should be emphasized in lieu of rules or attitudes? In fact, some of the critics even took the final step of associating realism with Nazism. A group of Roman Catholic scholars were particularly prone to strong criticisms of realism for its amorality.[13] Walter B. Kennedy, of Fordham University, for example, referred to realism in 1941 as a "goose-step philosophy."[14] Even the more restrained advocates of natural law, such as Harvard's Lon Fuller, associated the intellectual foundation of realism with totalitarianism.[15]

Given attacks such as these, what ambitious young scholar would dare call himself a legal realist? Clearly, after the mid-1930s, the realist movement gained few new disciples. In addition, some of the "old" realists began to bank the fires of their earlier convictions. Max Radin apologized for raising any possible inference in his writings that "ideas like wrong and right, or any ideas, are worthless or meaningless. . . ."[16] Jerome Frank, in his *Courts on Trial*, published in 1949, took great pains to tread lightly on the Catholic view of natural law,[17] and in the 1939 edition of *Law and the Modern Mind*, Frank went so far as to describe natural law as the "basis for modern civilization."[18] Finally, in 1940 Karl Llewellyn, the leading realist and principal prosopographer of the movement confessed what he believed to be the error of his past views. Alluding mainly to his *The Bramble Bush*, Llewellyn submitted that he was "ready to do open penance for any part I may have played" in popularizing the view that "the heart and core of jurisprudence" is something besides "right guidance."[19] With the leading realists so willing to surrender one of the movement's most important postulates, is it any wonder that the already splintering movement diffused even further? Most importantly, the commitment to empirical research was so identified by the legal community with realism that, when the realist movement was made suspect on the basis of its amorality, its empirical dimension could not be broken off and preserved.

The identification of realism with a "might-makes-right" philosophy was without any serious justification. None of the realists supported the Third Reich, and none of them believed that the mere study of legal (or illegal) behavior implied that the investigator endorsed that behavior. In fact, many of the realists were only too anxious to abandon secure places in academe and rush to the defense of democracy by serving in various New Deal capacities. If government service is a sign of patriotism, then Frank, Arnold, Douglas, Clark, and Oliphant—all realists—were patriots and not proto-Nazis. Moreover, one of the most important intellectual concerns of the realists in the 1930s had been to demonstrate the nonempirical basis of various legal abstractions. By doing so, the realists believed they were working toward a more honest and more open democratic society. The fact that their critics in the 1930s did not acknowledge the realists' many services to the government and to democracy in general raises the possibility that part of the criticism was politically motivated. For example, one of the most vehement attacks on realism came from New York lawyer Raoul Desvernine, head of the "Legal Division" of the American Liberty League, a scurrilous anti-New Deal organization. In 1941 Desvernine recklessly charged that realism was "radically subversive of the American way of life."[20]

After Realism

To contend that legal realism was a casualty of World War II may be to render a premature obituary on this ill-defined movement.[21] In truth, many of the realists' views are still held (or once again held) by members of the legal community. Appellate judges frequently rely upon extra-legal sources and information; law schools still employ "cases and materials" texts; and most members of the legal community today share the realists' skepticism regarding the possibility of obtaining certainty in the law. But the commitment to empirical legal research, while slowly returning, is much less pronounced than it was in the thirties. Also, the debate between realists and antirealists that was waged in the law reviews in the thirties is now consigned to the dusty, bound volumes of the appropriate periodicals, seldom read any more except by a few curious legal historians. Realism might be said to linger in spirit, but as the vital movement that once prominently occupied the thoughts of the judiciary, the bar, and the law schools, it is no longer recognizable. Similarly, although contemporary legal culture still relies heavily upon extra-legal information, the unabashed devotion to data of the thirties has gone the way of realism.

Given the myriad of events portending legal consequences that have taken place since 1940, and given the brief buffer of time separating today from World War II, it is difficult to determine the jurisprudential mood of the last forty years. It may well be that future scholars will conclude that no dominant spirit for this period existed or that these years witnessed competing paradigms. In any event, succeeding generations of legal scholars interested in synthesizing the 1940-80 period will have to concern themselves with diverse matters such as the Warren Court's epoch-making individual rights cases, McCarthyism, the "Imperial Presidency," Watergate, the declining respect for authority in the sixties, the Vietnam War, the increasing concentration of economic power in the hands of multinational corporations, and, of course, the activities of legal educators and the legal profession itself.[22]

At present, the only single strong image I have of contemporary legal culture is that evoked by a picture on the cover of a 1977 issue of *Newsweek*. The traditional blindfolded matron is depicted with the scales of justice in one hand, while the other hand is clutching her forehead indicating a headache. The cover story is titled "Too Much Law?"[23] *Newsweek* has not been alone in suggesting this theme: in the last few years, other popular magazines and one short book on legal history have directed their attention at the allegedly excessive role of law and litigation in contemporary American life.[24]

These publications have claimed that America has too many law suits, too many laws hamstringing behavior, too much delay in the courts, too many lawyers, and perhaps even too much conflicting information.

In 1979 the country had almost five hundred thousand practicing lawyers, an increase of more than 50 percent since the midsixties. This is three times as many lawyers per capita as England and twenty times as many per capita as Japan. As lawyers have multiplied, so have laws, law suits, and court costs. In 1977 legislative bodies at all levels enacted about one hundred fifty thousand new laws. The case load of the federal courts rose by over 50 percent between 1969 and 1972, even after making a correction for the increase in the country's population during those years. Perhaps even more revealing is that fully four times as many suits are now filed yearly in California state courts as in the entire federal court system. Finally, legal fees are now costing the country more than $25 billion a year.[25]

If contemporary America, in fact, does have too much law, it is clear that this state of affairs did not occur overnight. It, in all likelihood, has been gaining force since the early years of the twentieth century, sparked particularly by the creation of independent regulatory commissions in the New Deal and the economic boom the country enjoyed from World War II to the early seventies. Given the pace and degree of the law's growth in the last generation. it is not surprising that some members of the legal professoriate have tried to bring a measure of order to legal doctrine. Just as law professors in the early twentieth century sought to impose order on the chaotic case law by developing legal encyclopedias, repertoires like the American Law Reports, and the codelike Restatement, so too have some law professors of the last two or three decades attempted to bring doctrinal order to American law.

Although no new, well-funded efforts to rival the Restatement have been produced in recent years, a great deal of talk about achieving rationality in legal doctrine has occurred. In the fifties, the *Harvard Law Review* began the still honored practice of inviting a distinguished legal authority to write a "Forward" to each year's *Review*. The term "Forward" was (and is) a misnomer; it is actually an extended comment upon selected aspects of the U.S.

Supreme Court's decisions of the past October Term. Throughout
the fifties and early sixties, the *Review*'s Forwards tended to sound
a singular note. They urged that appellate court decisions be based
upon the tenets of a philosophy that has since been characterized
as "reasoned elaboration."[26] Advocates of reasoned elaboration
admonished judges, particularly Supreme Court justices, to present
clear, detailed, and well-articulated rationale for their decisions.
Certainly, the Vinson Court, which in the late forties and early
fifties had relied excessively upon unsigned, *per curiam* opinions,
had engaged in an unfortunate practice and deserved to be criticized
for shirking the responsibility of providing the legal community
with substantive analyses of its decisions.[27] However, the advocates
of reasoned elaboration posited other, more controversial standards
for appellate decision making. They urged that decisions should
derive from "the maturing of collective thought," and that the
decisions should express the general "social preferences" of con
temporary society. A necessary corollary of these tenets was that an
appellate court should refrain from making any decision if the
members of the body were not in agreement with the social values
of the times or if society's "collective thought" had not matured
to the point at which it gave clear guidance to the judiciary.[28]

The advocates of reasoned elaboration were critical of the activism
of the U.S. Supreme Court in the late fifties and early sixties. Alexander Bickel, a law professor at Yale and a champion of reasoned
elaboration, was particularly hard on the Court for not practicing
the "passive virtues" of judicial self-restraint.[29] The "elaborationists"
were also critical of the few remaining legal realists for down-
playing the importance of the reasons given by judges for their
decisions. They also took the realists to task for their belief that
judicial decisions were more motivated by extra-legal factors than
by the taught tradition of the law.[30] The classic statement of the
reasoned elaborationist viewpoint was Herbert Wechsler's 1959
Holmes Lectures, "Toward Neutral Principles of Constitutional
Law,"[31] in which the author set forth standards for "principled"
decision making. The most important article of faith for Wechsler
was that judges must decide cases based upon "adequate neutrality
and generality," that the principles of law applied must be applicable to a variety of fact situations that "transcend the case at

hand."[32] The article concluded by discussing some past decisions of the Supreme Court in which the resort to neutral principles would have been warranted.[33] A small amount of irony can be found in Wechsler's call for neutral principles. In the period 1928-31, Wechsler was a student in the Columbia Law School, sympathetic to the curricular changes of the functional reformers.[34] Oliphant, Moore, Douglas, and the other leading functionalists at Columbia, later to be identified as among the leading legal realists, believed that all cases were unique and therefore, should be studied on their own terms and in appropriately specific social contexts. Furthermore, in 1940 Wechsler was one of the editors of *Cases and Materials on Criminal Law and Its Administration*, the book regarded as the best of the realist-inspired, social science-oriented law school casebooks.[35] So it appears that Wechsler had become an advocate of reasoned elaboration only after sluffing off his realism.

In the sixties, reasoned elaboration seemed out of harmony with the activism of the Warren Court. A stinging indictment of reasoned elaboration came in a 1971 law review article, authored by Federal Judge J. Skelly Wright.[36] Judge Wright criticized reasoned elaborationists like Bickel and Wechsler for their failure to appreciate the true contributions of the Warren Court's activism. He repudiated the institutional conservatism that he saw as the foundation for reasoned elaboration. Judge Wright's attack on reasoned elaboration is strongly reminiscent of Federal Judge Hutcheson's critique of the slot-machine theory of jurisprudence, published in the *Cornell Law Quarterly* over forty years earlier.[37]

The failure of the credo of reasoned elaboration to survive the sixties does not necessarily mean that all current efforts to bring coherence to American law are destined for a similar fate.[38] Yet, the present day confusion in legal culture will not easily bow to a single unitary paradigm. In the early twentieth century, a society in rapid flux saw its legal community look to myriad sources of information for guidance. Today, a society changing at an even faster rate has placed an unprecedented amount of trust in a legal community that is groping for coherence. On the fundamental question of whether modern American society's trust in today's legal community is warranted, the jury is still out.

Notes

1. John W. Johnson, "The Dimensions of Non-Legal Evidence in the American Judicial Process: The United States Supreme Court's Use of Extra-Legal Materials in the Twentieth Century" (Unpublished Ph.D. Dissertation: University of Minnesota, 1974), pp. 187-194.

2. See generally Alfred Kelly, "Clio and the Court: An Illicit Love Affair," *The Supreme Court Review* 119 (1965); Jacobus ten Broek, "Admissibility and Use by the United States Supreme Court of Extrinsic Aids in Constitutional Construction," 26 *California Law Review* 287, 437, 664 (1938) and 27 *California Law Review* 157, 399 (1939); John G. Wofford, "The Blinding Light: The Use of History in Constitutional Interpretation," 31 *University of Chicago Law Review* 502 (1964); William Anderson, "The Intention of the Framers: A Note on Constitutional Interpretation," 49 *American Political Science Review* 340 (1955); and Charles A. Miller, *The Supreme Court and the Uses of History* (Cambridge, Mass., 1969).

3. Quoted in Lester J. Mazor, "The Materials of Law Study: 1971," in Herbert L. Packer and Thomas Ehrlich, eds., *New Directions in Legal Education* (New York, 1972), pp. 319-320.

4. This phrase has been written and uttered so frequently that its origin is uncertain. See the discussion of the paradoxical legacy of realism in Robert Stevens, "Two Cheers for 1870: The American Law School," 5 *Perspectives in American History* 405, 543-548 (1971).

5. Robert M. Hutchins, "The Autobiography of an Ex-Law Student," 1 *University of Chicago Law Review* 511, 512-513 (1934).

6. Ibid., 516.

7. Robert W. Gordon, "J. Willard Hurst and the Common Law Tradition in American Legal Historiography," 10 *Law and Society Review* 9, 34 (1975).

8. Evidences of this new concern for empirical legal studies include: (1) the sociolegal history from the "Wisconsin school" of J. Willard Hurst; (2) "impact studies" of Supreme Court decisions by political scientists; and (3) the founding of the empirically oriented *Law and Society Review* in 1966. On the literature of Hurst and the Wisconsin school, see Gordon, "J. Willard Hurst and the Common Law Tradition in American Legal Historiography," 44-55; Ronald Eskin and Robert Hayden, "James Willard Hurst: A Bibliography," 10 *Law and Society Review* 325 (1976). The best of the impact studies are Stephen L. Wasby, *The Impact of the United States Supreme Court: Some Perspectives* (Homewood, Ill., 1970); and Theodore L. Becker, ed., *The Impact of Supreme Court Decisions* (New York, 1969).

9. Karl Llewellyn, "Some Realism About Realism—Responding to Dean Pound," 44 *Harvard Law Review* 1222, 1236-1237 (1931).

10. Karl Llewellyn, "A Realistic Jurisprudence—The Next Step," 30 *Columbia Law Review* 431, 464 (1930).

11. See my discussion, *supra*, chapter 6.

12. On the decline of realism during the late thirties and early forties, see esp. Edward A. Purcell, Jr., "American Jurisprudence Between the Wars: Legal Realism and the Crisis of Democratic Theory," 75 *American Historical Review* 424, 436-446 (1969). Purcell's account comes close to being definitive; much of my discussion follows his. See also G. Edward White, *Patterns of American Legal Thought* (Indianapolis, 1978), pp. 139-144.

13. Purcell, "American Jurisprudence Between the Wars," 439-440.

14. "Walter B. Kennedy," *My Philosophy of Law: Credos of Sixteen American Scholars* (Boston, 1941), pp. 151-152.

15. Lon L. Fuller, *The Law in Quest of Itself*, 2nd ed. (Boston, 1966), pp. 89, 122; see also Fuller, "Positivism and Fidelity to Law—A Reply to Professor Hart," 71 *Harvard Law Review* 630, 659 (1957).

16. Max Radin, "The Defense of an Unsystematic Science of Law," 51 *Yale Law Journal* 1269, 1275 (1942).

17. Jerome Frank, *Courts on Trial: Myth and Reality in American Justice* (Princeton, 1949), pp. 363-368.

18. Jerome Frank, *Law and the Modern Mind* (New York, 1939), xvii, xx.

19. Karl Llewellyn, "On Reading and Using the Newer Jurisprudence," 40 *Columbia Law Review* 581, 603 (1940).

20. Quoted in Purcell, "American Jurisprudence Between the Wars," 440.

21. On the lingering influence of realism, see esp. Calvin Woodard, "The Limits of Legal Realism: An Historical Perspective," in Packer and Ehrlich, eds., *New Directions in Legal Education*, pp. 331-384; Grant Gilmore, *The Ages of American Law* (New Haven, 1977), pp. 99-111; Stevens, "Two Cheers for 1870," 504-548.

22. Some of these subjects are treated perceptively in Paul L. Murphy, *The Constitution in Crisis Times, 1918-1969* (New York, 1972), pp. 248-485; Alan Reitman, ed., *The Pulse of Freedom: American Civil Liberties 1920-1970s* (New York, 1975), pp. 123-298; Joel Seligman, *The High Citadel: The Influence of Harvard Law School* (Boston, 1978), pp. 68-200; Jerold Auerbach, *Unequal Justice: Lawyers and Social Change in Modern America* (New York, 1976), pp. 231-306; and G. Edward White, *The American Judicial Tradition: Profiles of Leading American Judges* (New York, 1976), pp. 317-368.

23. Jerold K. Footlick et al., "Too Much Law?" 89 *Newsweek* 42 (January 10, 1977).

24. See "Those #*X!!! Lawyers," 111 *Time* 56 (April 10, 1978); Jerold S. Auerbach, "A Plague of Lawyers," 253 *Harper's* 37 (October 1976); "Trouble with Lawyers," 178 *New Republic* 5 (May 20, 1978); Laurence H. Tribe, "Too Much Law, Too Little Justice: An Arguement for Delegalizing America," 244 *The Atlantic* 25 (July 1979); and Gilmore, pp. 104-111. Gilmore concludes his brief volume with a paraphrase of Holmes: "The worse the society, the more law there will be. In Hell there will be nothing but law, and due process will be meticulously observed." Gilmore, p. 111.

25. The statistics in this paragraph are drawn from Laurence Tribe's *Atlantic* article, "Too Much Law, Too Little Justice," 25.

26. The phrase "reasoned elaboration" was coined in 1958 by Harvard law professors Henry M. Hart and Albert M. Sacks. They alluded to it in their widely used but unpublished set of law school course materials, "The Legal Process." A thorough treatment of the reasoned elaboration perspective is White, *Patterns of American Legal Thought*, pp. 136-163. Much of my discussion here follows White's account. The major "texts" of reasoned elaboration include Louis Jaffe, "Forward to the Supreme Court, 1950 Term," 65 *Harvard Law Review* 107 (1951); Albert Sacks, "Forward to the Supreme Court, 1953 Term," 68 *Harvard Law Review* 96 (1954); Henry Hart, "The Supreme Court, 1958 Term—Forward: The Time Chart of the Justices," 73 *Harvard Law Review* 84 (1959); Herbert Wechsler, "Toward Neutral Principles of Constitutional Law," 73 *Harvard Law Review* 1 (1959); Erwin Griswold, "The Supreme Court, 1959 Term—Forward: Of Time and Attitudes—Professor Hart and Judge Arnold," 74 *Harvard Law Review* 81 (1960); Alexander Bickel, "The Supreme Court, 1960 Term—Forward: The Passive Virtues," 75 *Harvard Law Review* 40 (1961); Robert G. McCloskey, "The Supreme Court, 1961 Term—Forward: The Reapportionment Case," 76 *Harvard Law Review* 54 (1962); and Philip Kurland, "The Supreme Court, 1963 Term—Forward: 'Equal in Origin and Equal in Title to the Legislative and Executive Branches of the Government,' " 78 *Harvard Law Review* 143 (1964).

27. Jaffe, "Forward to the Supreme Court, 1950 Term," 108-113; Sacks, "Forward to The Supreme Court, 1953 Term," 103.

28. See generally the articles cited, *supra*, note 26. See also the discussion of G. Edward White, *Patterns of American Legal Thought*, pp. 144-150.

29. Bickel, "The Supreme Court, 1960 Term," passim.

30. White, *Patterns of American Legal Thought*,pp. 142-144.

31. 73 *Harvard Law Review* 1 (1959).

32. Ibid., 15,17.

33. Ibid., 20-35.

34. Seligman, pp. 51-52.

35. At least this is the assessment made by David Riseman in his review of the book. See Riesman, "Law and Social Science: A Report on Michael and Wechsler's Classbook on Criminal Law and Administration," 50 *Yale Law Journal* 636, 653 (1940).

36. J. Skelly Wright, "Professor Bickel, the Scholarly Tradition, and the Supreme Court," 84 *Harvard Law Review* 769 (1971).

37. Joseph Hutcheson, "The Judgment Intuitive: The Function of the 'Hunch' in Judicial Decision," 14 *Cornell Law Quarterly* 274 (1929).

38. One attempt at fashioning a unitary paradigm has been offered by the newly established *Journal of Legal Studies*. The *Journal*'s editor, Richard Posner, articulated the purpose of this periodical in an early issue: "The aim of the *Journal* is to encourage . . . systematic observation of how the legal system operates in fact and to discover and explain the recurrent patterns in the observation—the 'laws' of the system." Quoted in Gilmore, p. 146, note 11. This curious blend of the empiricism of the realists and the formalism of Langdell's legal science has been labeled the "new conceptualism" by Gilmore. See pp. 107-110; pp. 146-147, note 11.

BIBLIOGRAPHICAL ESSAY

Extensive annotation precludes the need for a long and copious bibliographical commentary. However, a few statements about those sources I found particularly helpful are in order.

For the reasons noted in the "Introduction," this study of American legal history does not include many detailed discussions of court cases. Nevertheless, to assess the impact of various forms of extra-legal information upon the judiciary, I took a 10 percent random sample of the decisions of the United States Supreme Court between 1925 and 1970. I read these cases carefully, along with the accompanying briefs of counsel and any *amicus curiae* briefs. In addition, I scrutinized the two dozen or so "great" cases of the twentieth century, looking for any indications that those decisions were predicated upon extra-legal information. Curiously, I found that almost three-quarters of the extra-legal evidence cited by the Supreme Court was suggested to the justices by the attorneys arguing the cases. State appellate courts in the early twentieth century appeared to rely less frequently upon extra-legal information than did the U.S. Supreme Court. Yet, I cannot insist upon this point because I have only dipped unsystematically into the reports of the highest courts of a few states, namely, New York, Massachusetts, Wisconsin, and South Carolina.

Since extra-legal information per se was of little consequence to the country's legal system before the twentieth century, few writers have sought to chronicle its incidence. The exceptions to this rule include Alfred H. Kelly, "Clio and the Court: An Illicit Love Affair," *The Supreme Court Review* 119 (1965); Charles A. Miller, *The Supreme Court and the Uses of History* (Cambridge, Mass., 1969); Marie Carolyn Klinkhamer, "The Use of History in the Supreme Court, 1789-1835," 36 *University of Detroit Law Journal* 553 (1959); Jacobus ten Broek, "Admissibility and Use by the United States Supreme Court of Extrinsic Aids in Constitutional Construction," 26 *California Law Review* 287, 437, 664 (1938) and 27 *California Law Review* 157, 399 (1939); Charles W. Pierson, "*The Federalist* in the Supreme Court," 33 *Yale Law Journal* 728 (1924); Richard J. Hoffman, "Classics in the Courts of the United States, 1790-1800," 22 *American Journal of Legal History* 55 (1978); and Max Radin, "Sources of Law—New and Old," 1 *Southern California Law Review* 42 (1928).

Although extra-legal information had little impact on American courts in the nineteenth century, the appellate judiciary was not isolated from extra-legal influence and the general *zietgeist*. A number of scholars have examined the effects of laissez-faire ideology and social Darwinist principles on the bench. In this connection, the best studies are Arnold Paul, *Conservative Crisis and the Rule of Law: Attitudes of Bench and Bar, 1887-1895* (Ithaca, N.Y., 1960); Clyde E. Jacobs, *Law Writers and the Courts: The Influence of Thomas M. Cooley, Christopher G. Tiedeman, and John F. Dillon Upon American Constitutional Law* (Berkeley, 1954); Benjamin R. Twiss, *Lawyers and the Constitution: How Laissez-Faire Came to the Supreme Court* (Princeton, 1942); Alan Jones, "Thomas M. Cooley and 'Laissez-Faire Constitutionalism': A Reconsideration," 53 *Journal of American History* 759 (1967); and Barton J. Bernstein, "*Plessy* v. *Ferguson*: Conservative Sociological Jurisprudence," 48 *Journal of Negro History* 196 (1963). An excellent discussion of the intellectual environment that reinforced the "fellow-servant rule" of tort liability is Lawrence M. Friedman and Jack Ladinsky, "Social Change and the Law of Industrial Accidents," 67 *Columbia Law Review* 51 (1967).

The chapter on nineteenth-century American legal history in this study benefited from a handful of superior general works. Charles Warren's *History of the Harvard Law School and of Early Legal Conditions in America*, 2 vols. (New York, 1908), is dated but still useful. Two of J. Willard Hurst's works, *The Growth of American Law: The Law Makers* (Boston, 1950) and *Law and Social Order in the United States* (Ithaca, N.Y. 1977), provided general background and frequent substantive insights. The collection *Essays in Nineteenth Century American Legal History* (Westport, Conn., 1976), edited by Wythe Holt, Jr., also offered much of value. The best thematic work on nineteenth-century American law is Morton J. Horwitz's *The Transformation of American Law, 1780-1860* (Cambridge, Mass., 1977). Horwitz's thesis regarding the unique "instrumental" function of law in the nineteenth century is open to question, but his grasp of the interface between legal doctrine and social concerns is sure.

As discussed in the text, no adequate synthetic legal history of twentieth-century America exists. Friedman's *A History of American Law* (New York, 1973) and Grant Gilmore's *The Ages of American Law* (New Haven, 1977) are suggestive of some important issues but are too brief in their coverage. Bernard Schwartz's *The Law in America: A History* (New York, 1974) is more detailed than either Friedman or Gilmore, but his book fails to relate legal changes to general social concerns. Hurst's *Law and the Social Order in the United States* is very strong on the social and economic influences on the structure and functions of legal agencies. As much as I respect and have profited from the writings of Hurst and the "Wisconsin school" of legal history, I believe that in their quest to write a "social history of the law," they have unduly slighted the role of ideas in spawning legal changes.

In contrast to the absence of satisfactory synthetic treatments of twentieth-century legal history, the overlapping field of constitutional history is well represented in the scholarly literature. The twentieth-century chapters in Kelly and Winfred Harbison, *The American Constitution: Its Origins and Development*, 5th ed. (New York, 1976), and Robert G. McCloskey, *The American Supreme Court* (Chicago, 1960), provide good analyses of leading constitu-

tional decisions of the U.S. Supreme Court. In addition, besides
providing case analysis, Paul L. Murphy's *Constitution in Crisis
Times, 1918-1969* (New York, 1972) offers thoughtful discussions
of the social and political forces that impinged on constitutional
law in this century.

A host of specific twentieth-century legal themes have come in
for discussion by historians, political scientists, and law professors.
It would take an entire essay to list even the best of these works.
However, the following specialized studies proved most useful to
me in pursuing this project: Clement Vose, *Constitutional Change:
Amendment Politics and Supreme Court Litigation Since 1900*
(Lexington, Mass., 1972); Vose, "The National Consumers' League
and the Brandeis Brief," 1 *Midwest Journal of Political Science*
267 (1962); Paul L. Rosen, *The Supreme Court and Social Science*
(Urbana, Ill., 1972); Murphy, *The Meaning of Freedom of Speech:
First Amendment Freedoms from Wilson to FDR* (Westport, Conn.,
1972); G. Edward White, *Patterns of American Legal Thought*
(Indianapolis, 1978); and Chester A. Newland, "Legal Periodicals
and the United States Supreme Court," 3 *Midwest Journal of
Political Science* 58 (1959).

The history of formal legal education in the twentieth century is a
topic treated at length in the text. The literature on this subject is
large but of uneven quality. The best general examination of American legal education is Robert Stevens, "Two Cheers for 1870: The
American Law School," 5 *Perspectives in American History* 405
(1971). Also useful are two older articles by Brainerd Currie, "The
Materials of Law Study, Parts I and II," 3 *Journal of Legal Education* 331 (1951), and "Non-Legal Materials in the Law School, Part
III," 8 *Journal of Legal Education* 1 (1955); the latter of Currie's
articles is particularly good on the twenties and thirties. On the
nineteenth century, Warren's old *History of the Harvard Law
School and of Early Legal Conditions in America* is a standard
source. The changes in legal education in the late nineteenth century
are placed in the context of general changes in American universities
by Burton J. Bledstein's *The Culture of Professionalism: The Middle Class and the Development of Higher Education in America*
(New York, 1976). The two Carnegie Foundation studies of the
World War I period—Joseph Redlich's *The Common Law and the*

Case Method in American University Law Schools (New York, 1914) and Alfred Z. Reed, *Training for the Public Profession of the Law* (New York, 1921)—provide a plethora of information on the status of legal education in the early twentieth century. The best primary source on the crucial pedagogical issues raised by legal educators in the twenties is Herman Oliphant, ed., *Summary of Studies in Legal Education by the Faculty of Columbia University* (New York, 1928). Other details on the history of American legal education can be found in the studies of individual law schools; these now number about twenty. I found the most useful law school histories to be Warren's *History of the Harvard Law School*; Arthur Sutherland, *The Law at Harvard: A History of Ideas and Men, 1817-1967* (Cambridge, Mass., 1967); Julius Goebel, Jr., et al., *A History of the School of Law, Columbia University* (New York, 1955); and Joel Seligman, *The High Citadel: The Influence of Harvard Law School* (Boston, 1978). Although informative, law school histories tend to be too celebratory, too parochial, and not sufficiently analytical. Only Seligman's brief history of the Harvard Law School does not fall prey to these criticisms.

A related topic, the history of the legal profession in the twentieth century, also receives some attention in the text. Until recently, studies of the legal profession have suffered from many of the same failings as the law school histories. However, with the publication of Jerold S. Auerbach's *Unequal Justice: Lawyers and Social Change in Modern America* (New York, 1976) and William R. Johnson's *Schooled Lawyers: A Study in the Clash of Professional Cultures* (New York, 1978), two books now exist on the twentieth-century legal profession that have succeeded in placing American lawyers within the stream of social and political history. In addition, both of these studies have subjected lawyers and their professional associations to stringent criticisms for a variety of activities and attitudes. Auerbach focuses on elite attorneys and their national associations, and Johnson centers his attention on Wisconsin lawyers. The treatments of Auerbach and Johnson may be subject to criticism for selective use of evidence and strained conclusions, but they are still the best studies of the twentieth-century legal profession. Robert Wiebe's *The Search for Order, 1877-1920* (New York, 1967) has a very good chapter placing the activities of the American bar around the turn of the century within the context of a general movement among American professions in the period to raise standards and limit access to professional membership.

Much of the best writing on twentieth-century American legal history has been accomplished by biographers. The most useful biographies for my purposes were Alpheus T. Mason's two books on Louis Brandeis, *Brandeis: Lawyer and Judge in the Modern State* (Princeton, 1933) and *Brandeis: A Free Man's Life* (New York, 1946); William Twining's *Karl Llewellyn and the Realist Movement* (London, 1973); and David Wigdor's *Roscoe Pound: Philosopher of Law* (Westport, Conn., 1974). Other good biographical information on important twentieth-century legal figures is provided in White, *The American Judicial Tradition: Profiles of Leading American Judges* (New York, 1976); John T. Noonan, Jr., *Persons and Masks of the Law: Cardozo, Holmes, Jefferson, and Wythe as Makers of the Masks* (New York, 1976); and John Semonche, *Charting the Future: The Supreme Court Responds to a Changing Society, 1890-1920* (Westport, Conn., 1978). Two splendid autobiographies—Samuel Williston's *Life and Law* (Boston, 1940) and William O. Douglas's *Go East, Young Man: The Early Years* (New York, 1974)—also offer many insights into the legal mind of the early twentieth century.

Rather than drawing extensively from private papers or correspondence, this study has emphasized the published writings of the leading legal figures of the period. To perform a thorough survey of the private papers of the principal representatives of the informational paradigm would have added years to this project. The published writings of the leading lawyers, judges, and law professors of the period are voluminous enough as it is. One advantage of stressing published sources is that it permits examination of the most considered and, presumably, most responsible ideas of the principals involved.

The thinking of the most profound and influential members of the early twentieth-century legal profession can be found in the law review literature. Particularly valuable for my purposes were the *Yale Law Journal*, the *Harvard Law Review*, the *Columbia Law Review*, and the *University of Chicago Law Review*. For understanding the debate over pedagogy and legal realism in the twenties and thirties, law reviews are the essential sources. Book length polemics by legal professors, lawyers, and judges are also important sources of ideas. The best of this genre include Jerome Frank's *Law and the Modern Mind* (New York, 1930) and *Courts on Trial: The Myth and Reality in American Justice* (New York, 1949); Karl Llewellyn's *The Bramble Bush: Some Lectures on Law and Its Study* (New York, 1930); Oliver Wendell Holmes's *Collected Legal Papers* (Washington, 1920); Benjamin Cardozo's *Nature of the Judicial Process* (New Haven, 1921); and Thurman Arnold's *Fair Fights and Foul* (New York, 1955) and *The Symbols of Government* (New York, 1962). Legal treatises on specialized subjects—such as Holmes's *The Common Law* (Boston, 1881), Williston's *The Law of Contracts*, 4 vols. (New York, 1920), and Ernst Freund's *The Police Power, Public Policy and Constitutional Rights* (Chicago, 1904) and *Standards of American Legislation: An Estimate of Restrictive and Constructive Factors* (Chicago, 1917)—occasionally provide instructive commentary on general legal or philosophical issues. Louis Brandeis, a central figure for this study, did not publish any single compendium of his legal thought, but he left an enduring record of his ideas on law and society in his Supreme Court opinions; Alexander M. Bickel's *The Unpublished Opinions of Mr. Justice Brandeis: The Supreme Court at Work* (Chicago, 1967) also offers revealing glimpses into Brandeis's brilliant legal thinking.

One of the most impressive, albeit somewhat narrow, achievements of the legal profession in the early twentieth century was the creation of research tools that eventually came to serve as "new sources" of the law. This phenomenon is intelligently discussed in Radin's "Sources of Law—New and Old"; William D. Lewis, "History of the American Law Institute and the First Restatement of the Law: How We Did It," in American Law Institute ed., *Restatement in the Courts* (St. Paul, 1945), pp. 1-23; Nathan Crystal, "Codification and the Rise of the Restatement Movement" (Unpublished essay, 1978); and Herbert F. Goodrich, "The Story of the American Law Institute," *Washington Law Quarterly* 283 (1951). The rows and rows of elegantly bound volumes of *Corpus Juris Secundum*, *American Jurisprudence*, *American Law Reports*, and, especially, the *Restatement* in the main reading room of any major law library provide a silent but powerful testimony to the significance of these research tools.

The legal realist movement of the twenties and thirties is of continuing interest to legal historians. The main statements of the realists can be found in the law reviews and the polemical literature previously noted. The law reviews of the interwar years also carried scores of antirealist articles. Regrettably, no comprehensive scholarly treatment of legal realism exists—this is one of the most glaring lacunae in the literature of American legal history. The best examination of the intellectual climate of opinion that gave rise to realism is Morton White's *Social Thought in America: The Revolt Against Formalism* (New York, 1949). A competent analytical treatment of some dimensions of legal realism is Wilfrid E. Rumble, Jr., *American Legal Realism: Skepticism, Reform, and the Judicial Process* (Ithaca, N.Y., 1968). Rumble, however, limits his examination of realism to the ideas of the men on Llewellyn's 1931 list of realists and fails to treat the historical twists and turns in realism. Twining's *Karl Llewellyn and the Realist Movement*, besides being the best biography of any of the realists, contains about one hundred pages of outstanding historical exposition and analysis of realism. However, because Twining's focus is on Llewellyn's ideas and career at Columbia and the University of Chicago, his book gives short shrift to the wide range of realist activities, especially at Yale in the thirties. The best treatments of the relationship between legal realism and American life and thought are Edward A. Purcell, Jr., "American Jurisprudence Between the Wars: Legal Realism and the Crisis of Democratic Theory," 75 *American Historical Review* 424 (1969); G. Edward White, "Sociological Jurisprudence to Realism: Jurisprudence and Social Change in Early Twentieth Century America," 58 *Virginia Law Review* 999 (1972); and Eugene V. Rostow, "The Realist Tradition in American Law," in Arthur Schlesinger, Jr., and Morton White, eds., *Paths of American Thought* (Boston, 1963), pp. 203-218. The decline of legal realism during the 1940s and its replacement by other strains of legal thinking are treated in Calvin Woodard, "The Limits of Legal Realism: A Historical Perspective," 54 *Virginia Law Review* 689 (1968); sections of Stevens's essay "Two Cheers for 1870"; and G. Edward White, "The Evolution of Reasoned Elaboration: Jurisprudential Criticism and Social Change," 59 *Virginia Law Review* 279 (1973). As White clearly illustrates, the dominant threads of legal thinking in the fifties and early sixties were woven by law professors writing in the *Harvard Law Review*'s annual "Forwards." Another important statement of the postrealist philosophy is Herbert Wechsler's famous Holmes Lecture, "Toward Neutral Principles of Constitutional Law," published in 73 *Harvard Law Review* 1 (1959). By the early seventies, a few members of the legal community were once again sounding like realists; this is apparent in an essay such as Federal Judge J. Skelly Wright's "Professor Bickel, the Scholarly Tradition, and the Supreme Court," 84 *Harvard Law Review* 769 (1971).

Since World War II, a great deal has transpired in American legal history. It is, perhaps, too soon to expect ambitious synthetic treatments of legal culture for the recent past. Future scholars interested in the years 1940-80 will benefit from the accounts of the modern period in Murphy, *The Constitution in Crisis Times*; Alan Reitman, ed., *The Pulse of Freedom: American Civil Liberties 1920-1970s* (New York, 1975); Seligman, *The High Citadel*; Auerbach, *Unequal Justice*; White, *The American Judicial Tradition*; and McCloskey, *The Modern Supreme Court* (Cambridge, Mass., 1972).

INDEX

Restatement of the Law, 58-61, 67-68,
70n, 152, 158. *See also* American
Law Institute
Revolutionary casebooks. *See*
Casebooks, revolution in
Richards, H. S., 59
Riesman, David, 113, 152, 164n
Riis, Jacob, 129
Ritchie v. *Wayman*, 37
Roberts, Owen J., 38
Robinson, Edwin, 149n
Robinson, James Harvey, 125
Rockefeller Foundation, 108
Rodell, Fred, 133, 149n
Roosevelt, Franklin D., 38, 71n, 104,
109, 135, 139. *See also* New Deal
Russell Sage Foundation, 37

Sacks, Albert M., 163n. Work: "The
Legal Process" (with Henry M.
Hart, Jr.), 163n
Schecter Poultry v. *United States*, 139
Schubert, Glendon, 119n
"Scope and Purpose of Sociological
Jurisprudence" (Pound), 130
*Selection of Cases on the Law of
Contracts* (Langdell), 23. *See also*
Casebooks
Separate but equal. *See Plessy* v.
Ferguson
Shanks, Carrol M., 115n
Shaw, Lemuel, 17-18. *See also* em-
ployers' liability; Fellow servant
rule
Sinclair, Upton, 31. Work: *The Jungle*,
31. *See also* Progressivism
Slaughterhouse Cases, 13
Smith, Young B., 100, 113, 115n-116n
Social Darwinism, 13, 129
Socialism, 29, 33, 75, 91n, 135
Social sciences: in casebooks, 111-113;
in Columbia Law School's
functional curriculum, 96-100; at
Harvard Law School, 107; at Johns
Hopkins University, 101-102; and
legal realism, 132-133, 136-144
passim; in recent years, 152-154;
use by Louis Brandeis, 30-36, 39-
46; at Yale Law School, 102-106.

See also Empirical research;
Extra-legal authorities
Sociological jurisprudence: as
antecedent to legal realism,
123-128, 135, 149n; and
Progressivism, 129-130; and World
War I, 130-131. *See also* Extra-
legal authorities; Pound, Roscoe
Socratic dialogue (Socratic method),
22-24. *See also* Case method;
Langdell, Christopher Columbus
"Some Realism About Realism" (Frank
and Llewellyn), 135-136
Southern California Law Review, 54
Spencer, Herbert, 13
Statistics. *See* Empirical research
Statutory construction: American rule,
80; British rule, 80; definition of,
52; derogation canon in, 76-77; in
early twentieth century, 76-87, 89n;
increase in, 53, 65; in legal
education, 97; in modern period,
152; plain meaning rule of, 76-77
Statutory interpretation. *See* Statutory
Construction
Stettler v. *O'Hara*, 46n
Stone, Harlan F., 44, 64-65, 96
Story, Joseph, 18, 19, 21, 22, 74. Work:
*Commentaries on the Constitution
of the United States*, 19
Straight, Mrs. Willard, 37. *See also*
National Consumers' League
Struggle for Judicial Supremacy
(Jackson), 139
Sturges, Wesley, 133, 137
Summary of Studies in Legal Education
(Oliphant), 98. *See also* Columbia
University Law School, functional
curriculum at
Sumner, William Graham, 13
*Supreme Court and the Minimum
Wage* (National Consumers'
League), 38
Survey, 129. *See also* Kellogg, Paul
Swan, Thomas, 67
Swift v. *Tyson*, 63

Taft, William Howard, 41, 64
Taney, Roger, 18

About the Author

JOHN W. JOHNSON is Associate Professor of History at Clemson, South Carolina. His articles have appeared in journals such as *The Historian, The Indian Journal of American Studies,* and *The Detroit College of Law Review.*